Eccles Cakes

An Odd Tale of Survival

Jonathan Fryer

for Ismael Pordeus Jr

who encouraged me to write it

Other Books by Jonathan Fryer

History
The Great Wall of China
Soho in the Fifties and Sixties
Fuelling Kuwait's Development
Kurdistan: A Nation Emerges

Biography
Isherwood
Dylan
The Sitwells (with Sarah Bradford and John Pearson)
George Fox and the Children of the Light
Eye of the Camera
Wilde
André & Oscar
Robbie Ross

Other
Brussels as Seen by Naif Artists (with Rona Dobson)
Food for Thought

Part One

INSIDE

Everything is green. I am alone in the room, and there is silence, except for the sound of birds cheeping in the garden. Dust particles are jumping around in the rays of sunlight that are streaming in through the leaded bay window, beyond which I can just make out a summer fuzz of lawn and trees. A heavy brocade cloth, bottle green with a Paisley design picked out in gold thread, covers a round table, tassels hanging down from the table's edge. Exactly in the middle of the table is a glass bowl, filled with fruit made of porcelain. I reach out and touch one of the green china apples: hard and cold, yet magical. I like this place and feel safe here, but this is not where I live.

The district nurse stifles a laugh as she comes into the room, a bottle of disinfectant and some cotton wool in her hand. Perhaps she thinks I might drop and break one of the magical pieces of fruit if she startles me. She gestures silently to a straight-backed chair by the side of the table. I climb up onto it and sit rigid but unafraid, without saying a word.

'This will sting a bit,' she says softly. And yes, it does sting, as she carefully wipes the blood away from the puncture at the left side of my mouth. This was caused when I tripped back at the house I live in while helping the daily, Mrs Warburton, carry washed cutlery

*through from the kitchen into the dining room; I fell flat on my face
and a fork pierced my cheek. As she was alone in the house with me
at the time, Mrs Warburton had rushed me to the district nurse, who
lived round the corner. She must then have gone straight back to our
house, to wait for my adoptive mother Rosemary Fryer to return
home from golf, because she is not there with me in this quiet, green
room now.*

*I am three, and this is my first memory. The scar from the fork
will remain at the left side of my mouth until well into my 20s, when
somehow it just fades away, then disappears.*

* * *

About 18 months earlier, on 28 November 1951, at Eccles Parish
Church, the Vicar, Rev T. W. Taylor, christened me Jonathan
Harold. The Jonathan I have always liked, since I was old enough to
have such opinions, but I resented the Harold bitterly. That was
mainly because it marked me as the property of my adoptive father,
Harold Fryer, but also because the name was redolent of the
Victorian age – rather appropriately, as Harold Fryer was conceived
in December 1900 as Queen Victoria lay dying at Osborne. For a
small child in the 1950s, the Victorian era was like some monstrous
past, casting its long, dark shadow over the 20th Century. After
Harold Macmillan became Prime Minister in 1957, I was told I
should be proud to bear the name Harold, but on the contrary by
about that time for me it was starting to signify shame.

At the tea after the christening ceremony back in November 1951
I reportedly sat up and grabbed a piece of cake from a passing plate
and pushed it into my face. Well, I was one-and-a-half years old,
more of a toddler than a baby, though I remember nothing of this.
Sometimes I wonder if Harold and Rosemary (as I call them now,
but never would have dared to while they were alive) prayed at the
church that day, but I doubt it, as both were agnostics, though she
preferred to call herself a 'free thinker'. I suppose they went through
with the service because that was what people in post-War England
were meant to do, just as a married couple were meant to have
children, ideally one girl and one boy. Four years older than me, my

2

sister Hilary was also adopted, though not from the same birth mother.

As a memento of the christening I was given a silver napkin ring, which was kept polished but unused in a small cupboard in the sideboard in the dining room, along with a similar one that had been given to Hilary. I was also allocated three godparents: a pair of the Fryers' bridge partners, called Jack and Joan, and Rosemary's best friend, Ruth Hall, always referred to as 'Auntie Ruth'. Ruth had worked with Rosemary when they were both hospital nurses during the brief period when Rosemary was in employment in the late 1930s and for part of the Second World War. Ruth was a spinster, who lived with an obese handicapped maiden aunt and two snappy dachshunds in a semi-detached house in Middleton. She said more than once that she could never understand why Rosemary had married – and as I grew older, neither could I. Indeed, the reality of wedlock to her considerably older second cousin Harold must have come as something of a shock to her, as soon after the wedding in 1936 she volunteered to join an ambulance unit in the Spanish civil war, amazingly on the Republican side, given her later political views. But she was rejected when they discovered she was newly-wed.

* * *

Chatsworth Road, where I was taken to live after my adoption, used to provide one of the entrances to an estate that had belonged to the Egerton family, the Earls of Ellesmere, subsequently Dukes of Sutherland. All the roads in the area were named after ducal or other aristocratic families: Westminster, Sandwich and so on. The first late 19th Century houses built in Ellesmere Park were imposing residences with substantial grounds, but the development along Chatsworth Road was built later and most of the houses were notably smaller, though still mainly detached. When I was very young there was a Lodge at the beginning of Chatsworth Road and a wooden barrier barred entry to all but residents and bona fide visitors, though the barrier was removed when the local Council adopted the road; it was then properly surfaced, at least until the houses ran out at No.

3

39, after which it turned into a gravel track that ran across open fields and under a bridge through a raised disused railway line, all the way to Swinton. There were also fields behind the houses at the bottom end of Chatsworth Road, including ours at No. 35, and there was a pond in the middle of these fields, where a pike preyed on tiddlers and frogs spawned; you could collect tadpoles just by scooping them out of the smelly water with a jam-jar and take them home, though they always died before they turned into frogs. Another unmade road, known as Puddly Lane, ran across these back fields to a further housing development and the local tennis club. The lane was regularly recovered with cinders, yet still big puddles habitually formed each time it rained, and the water would splash loudly underneath cars, no matter how slowly they were driven.

No. 35 was the first of three identical detached houses built in a row, though subsequent owners have extended it so considerably that today it is almost unrecognisable. When I was little it resembled the sort of house I would build with my Bayko Building Set. It had a square façade, with a small porch at the front door and a large kitchen window looking out over the front garden. Under the stairs in the hall there was a walk-in cupboard known as the Bogey Hole, where coats and the hoover, as well as the green felt-covered bridge table with folding legs and various boxes of surplus china were kept. This would have made a perfect den – it even had a frosted window at the back looking out onto the side garden – but we children were told that the Bogey Man lived in there and I used to shudder just opening the door to grab a coat before I shut it again quickly.

A door from the kitchen led into the panelled dining room, which was all painted cream and had a picture rail that ran round three walls. Double doors at one side of the dining room connected to the lounge, where a coal fire blazed in winter and a chunky three piece suite dominated the room. Every so often, a coal lorry would arrive in the road outside, and men with dirty faces and hemp sacking over their necks and backs would struggle in carrying bags of coal to fill the metal-lined wooden former seaman's chest that stood by the fire and to top up the coal-store that was situated next to the house's back door.

The dining room had French windows opening out onto a veranda, from which two steps led down into the substantial back garden. At some stage a gate was built into the hedge right at the back of the garden, giving access to the fields. Unlike the houses at No. 37 and No. 39, No. 35 had a lawn that ran all the way down one side of the house linking the front and back gardens, all of which required the services of a gardener who cycled over twice a week to keep everything neat and tidy. For my first few years there was a wooden swing in one corner, but one winter when there was a lot of snow the wood rotted and the swing fell apart.

On the other side of the house, next to the indented kitchen porch, was the coal-store, where anthracite for the Aga in the kitchen was kept along with the coal for the fire. Once I was given a tortoise and when winter came, Harold put it in a shoebox in the coal-store to hibernate. But when we opened up the box the following spring we discovered that the tortoise had suffocated on the black coal dust. I buried it in a hole that I dug at the bottom of the garden, marking the spot with a twig, which soon fell over and was then thrown onto the 'rubbish pile', as the very basic compost heap in one corner of the garden was called. I had my own little plot to tend near where the tortoise was buried, down beyond the gooseberry bushes, and in summer I successfully grew tiny strawberries and lettuce there.

Further back from the coal-store, on the same side, was a garage that was attached to the house; it had a large window and a wooden work bench right at the back. Above the garage was a long room with windows at both ends and a sloping ceiling under the eaves, held up by a solid beam that had to be carefully avoided or else you would crack your head. The neighbours at No. 37 used their room over the garage to store large cardboard boxes full of tinned foods bought wholesale – an economy measure that Harold considered beneath contempt. But at No. 35, the room over the garage was where I slept. The floorboards were painted shiny black and by the bed there was a small magenta rug that slipped about the floor as if it had a life of its own. The room was furnished, like the rest of the house, in dark, heavy reproduction furniture (Jacobean style, Harold claimed): a bed, a wardrobe, a dressing table and two chests of drawers, all of which cast eerie shadows from the late evening summer sunlight coming through the west-facing window when I went to bed. In winter, it was freezing cold, as there was no heating of any kind, and I could see my breath as clouds of steam when I poked my head out from under the bedclothes. Sometimes I would blow onto the cold window panes and then make drawings in the condensation.

* * *

Four times a day on weekdays during term time I would count the paving stones along Chatsworth Road as I went back and forth to my primary school, Branwood House, which was just round the corner from the Lodge. I was always careful not to tread on any of the cracks in between the paving stones as that would break an unwritten code and make me liable for some dreadful punishment from invisible spirits. I was aware that these spirits were all around, though you could not see them and no-one ever talked about them. Sometimes I could hear them whispering in the trees, but at other times their voices were chattering in an unknown language inside my head. The net result of my hopping between paving stones so not to offend these spirits was an ungainly gait and the occasional wobble as I tried to keep my balance as I strode along. Success over the entire few hundred metres left me with a warm sense of achievement. I sometimes got funny looks if I happened to pass an adult neighbour but I never told anyone what I was doing because this was one of my secrets.

Branwood House had been an imposing double-fronted private residence before being turned into a small private school, and in fact it has since been restored to residential use. Tall and wide, but oddly shallow, the building in the 1950s housed a class and a teacher in each room, apart from the bathrooms and the kitchen, where food was prepared for those children who lived too far away to go home for lunch. The bottom right-hand room housed the reception class – though I doubt whether that term was in use in those days – and above that was the final year form, taught by the Headmaster, Mr Firth, a tall, handsome but strict presence originating from Yorkshire, still quite young, who was rather intimidating to me as a small child, with his insistence on good manners and behaviour. 'Always raise your cap when you pass a lady in the street!' he instructed us boys. Did that include the daily cleaning ladies who worked in the houses of affluent families in Ellesmere Park, I wondered, and decided that it was safer to assume that it did. 'Always stand up when a teacher comes into the room!' was another Firth injunction, which meant that I kept one eye alert to any movement of the door, like a dog with one ear cocked while it sleeps. 'Raise your arm straight and high when you want to ask a question, or when you need to go to the bathroom!' That last command was issued in a tone that unmistakably suggested that well brought-up children should not need to go to the toilet during class-time, except in a real emergency.

I do not recall there being more than a dozen or so pupils in each class, boys and girls mixed, all white, of course, and mostly from Ellesmere Park, though there were always several Jewish children from Prestwich or even further afield. During winter, taxis would come for them early on a Friday afternoon before it started getting dark. Most of the other children thought this was a shameless wheeze to get out of classes, but I wondered if some monster might catch them and eat them if they failed to get home before the start of Shabbat. I had heard that Jews were in terrible danger and that millions of them had died not so long before, though I did not yet understand quite how or why. Anyway, the Jewish children at Branwood House tended to keep very much to themselves, so I never really got the chance to ask them.

I was a slow starter at primary school, mainly because I could not see what was written on the blackboard. This did not matter so much in the lower forms, where lessons were conducted with big cut-out letters and wooden blocks and large-print picture books, all of which I could see reasonably well. But in the higher forms it became a great inconvenience, and I would be told off for asking whoever was sitting next to me when I was no longer able to follow what was going on, 'What does it say on the blackboard?' They must have thought I was backward at learning to read, whereas I just could not make out the letters. Eventually I blurted out the problem and the school rather crossly wrote to the Fryers suggesting they take me to an optician's for an eye-test. Sure enough, it turned out that I had severe myopia, especially in the left eye, so by the age of seven or eight I was fitted out with my first pair of round NHS glasses, with very thick lenses, and my classmates started to tease me as 'specky four eyes'.

* * *

There is a large garden at the side of Branwood House, including a paved playground, where many of the other children chase balls around, though I am not interested in playing with my classmates and usually just sit on a step and day-dream. Sometimes I see my sister Hilary, who is also at the school, but she is four years older, which seems like an eternity to me, and she has her own group of friends.

On occasions, an attractive young woman walks past Branwood and stops by the gate for a while, watching the children playing. I do not notice her, or if I do, I think nothing of it. But she is looking out for me, to reassure herself that I am all right.

She is my mother.

* * *

I always knew I was adopted, long before the meaning of the word was explained to me. Apparently, shortly after I arrived at No. 35 Hilary invited some of her little friends round to come and have a look at this new addition to the Fryer household. Years later Rosemary told me she had first seen me lying in a cardboard box, sneezing my head off, and had taken pity on me and brought me home. I very much doubt the existence of the cardboard box, which I suspect was just one of her many fantasies, but every summer through to my 20s was a nightmare of hay fever and associated asthma. As a child I asked Rosemary several times, with increasing agitation, who my real mother was, but she would say nothing more than 'nobody special', She claimed to have destroyed all paperwork related to the adoption, which had been arranged privately. Harold was angry when I turned to him to ask about my origins and he accused me of being ungrateful.

8

It never bothered me that I was a bastard, as everyone knew I must be, even in that era when illegitimacy was a matter of public shame. I would rather be the fruit of passion than of duty. I somehow knew I would never find out who my biological father was, but as the insecurity about my identity festered like a wound over the years I could console myself that the one thing that was certain was that my father was not Harold, who was anyway old enough to be a grandfather. He looked like an old man too, with his puffy bloodshot cheeks; stocky and not tall, his grey hair thinning at the temples, swept back to hide a bald patch.

'Nobody special,' Rosemary would repeat with irritation, when I asked yet again about my mother.

Yes, she is special, I think, as I try to imagine her. She is my mother.

* * *

All the neighbours were aware of my status, of course, as were all the members of the wider Fryer family, whose tentacles seemed to spread into every corner of Eccles and its surrounds. Harold was the seventh of 13 children, all of whom had miraculously survived the illnesses that swept Victorian and Edwardian England as well as the various wars. Most of the male siblings worked in the family business. This was a department store that had grown from a humble furniture shop, from which the oldest boys first delivered goods on a handcart. The brothers were known by the staff and even by many of the customers as Mr Harry, Mr Willie, Mr Harold and so on; that is even how they spoke about each other. The shop was founded by William Fryer, who had been born into poverty in 1867 in the village of Stanton in Derbyshire. As a youth he walked all the way to Manchester to seek his fortune. William had died long before I arrived on the scene, but his widow Martha (née Eyre) still lived in a towering Victorian house in Bindloss Avenue, Eccles (long since demolished to make way for a small housing estate). She was always referred to simply as Black Grandma, as she shared Queen Victoria's attitude towards mourning and the suitability of voluminous black gowns. She would sit in an armchair in the front parlour and I would

9

be taken to see her, pulled by my arm along a great long, dark corridor from the kitchen at the back of the house. She was well into her 80s and died before I could ever really get to know her. Besides, I was far more interested in the fact that outside the back door was a croquet lawn, though no-one ever played on it anymore.

Not all of William and Martha's seven daughters married, but all six sons did and most had produced children before Harold tied the knot in 1936 at the then unusually late age of 35. Before he died, on one of the rare occasions that I saw him after many years of bitter estrangement, he told me that he had once made Rosemary pregnant, but the child was stillborn and he had thrown the tiny corpse onto the fire. I found that very hard to believe, but far more convincing was his assertion that they never had sex again. Yet acquiring two children after the War meant that Harold and Rosemary now did not look too out of place among the fecund Fryers, though most of my Fryer adoptive cousins were 20 or even 30 years older than me, some already married and with families of their own. Although there were Fryers dotted all over Ellesmere Park, I did not see much of them. The fact that Harold maintained a simmering feud with most of his brothers did not exactly encourage casual interchange.

The one exception to this was the eldest son of William Fryer, named Harry, who also lived in Chatsworth Road until he and his wife Mary moved into a smarter house deeper inside Ellesmere Park. Harry was Chairman of the family business and had inherited the mantle of *paterfamilias* on William's death. In celebration of his status, he would take a party of all the numerous Fryer children and grandchildren to the circus at Belle Vue in Gorton every Christmas. I found the clowns sinister and worried about the well-being of the performing animals; after a couple of Christmases I said I did not want to go again. To me Harry resembled an older version of King Henry VIII, whom I knew from picture books. He was stout but not tall and was always smartly dressed in a three piece suit, with a gold watch attached to a chain in his fob pocket and a rose in his lapel. A pillar of the local masonic lodge, he was a genial host but also a great practical joker. Mary would try in vain to stop him teasing us children – including his grandson, Andrew Simmons, who many years later would like me become a foreign correspondent, but for Al

10

Jazeera TV – notably by giving us a dribbling glass to drink from: a beautiful cut glass beaker that had tiny holes in the side, so that it spilt drink onto your shirt or tie when you tried to take a sip from it. Harry had a white toy poodle, called Perry, who used to do a backwards somersault when proffered a spoonful of sherry. Despite Harry and Mary's hospitality I nonetheless always felt an outsider within the wider Fryer family, tolerated, even pitied, rather than loved. With Harold and Rosemary at No. 35, I felt like a cuckoo in the nest that had ended up there almost by accident, but unlike a cuckoo chick that soon outgrows his foster siblings and pushes them out, I felt tiny and gradually I shrank even more inside at the same time as I was getting physically bigger.

* * *

At the age of seven I began to withdraw from the physical environment around me and started to create a parallel universe through writing. My first short story, written in dark blue Quink on small shiny sheets of pale blue Basildon Bond notepaper as I sat at the desk in the dining room, was all about the cat that took up residence briefly at No. 35 and whose only name was Pussy. Pussy must have been a stray who wandered in one day and hung around long enough to realise this was not really the sort of home she was looking for, but in my story – long since lost – she set off on adventures that took her all the way to London. I realise now that the story of Dick Whittington must have influenced this narrative, though in my story there was no man nor even a boy involved. Just the cat. And I was the cat.

* * *

Until quite late in their lives, Harold and Rosemary did not really believe in abroad. In the early 1930s, she had gone to Portugal to stay on the estate of the wealthy family of a girl from her boarding school who had horses and a swimming pool, and one summer Rosemary's parents had taken her and her elder sister Doreen to the French Riviera. Nearly 20 years later she went to Germany to stay

11

with Doreen and her second husband, who was stationed with the occupying British army. But that was the sum of Rosemary's foreign travel until well into her 40s. For his part, Harold had his first taste of another country when he went on a trade mission to Czechoslovakia in 1946, the year he was President of the National Association of Furniture Makers. He brought back a beautiful heavy cut glass vase from this trip, which was regularly filled with flowers from the garden at No. 35. But he had been unimpressed with the Czechs in general. This was largely because glass-makers in Prague had said they were unable to make a bespoke glass jug for him to match a fragment he had brought with him from England; he was still moaning about it decades later. The fragment was a piece from a cut glass punch jug that the Bolsheviks had smashed when a family of white Russians had fled the country with their most precious belongings after the October Revolution of 1917, oddly ending up in Eccles. They had nonetheless been allowed to keep the massive solid silver punch jug frame and lid and its ladle, which were all studded with tiny precious stones, and these had passed to William and Martha Fryer, who had given assistance to the refugees when they arrived in England. These silver treasures – which also included a large, exquisite hexagonal sculpted silver platter by Fabergé – were passed down to Harold, and were wrapped up in old newspapers along with the rest of the household silver and packed into battered old brown leather suitcases to be deposited at the Westminster Bank in Eccles on the rare occasions that the house was going to be left empty. The fragment of glass from the broken punch jug was a constant reminder to Harold of the perfidy of the Communists, who in the 1950s were not only in control of central and eastern Europe, including Czechoslovakia, but were also strong in France and Italy. To him it seemed much wiser to stay at home in England.

It was therefore unusual that in the summer of 1957 Harold and Rosemary took Hilary and me to Jersey for a holiday. Perhaps flights had just started to St. Helier from Manchester Ringway airport or maybe Harold was given the trip in some trade promotion. Anyway, I was excited at the prospect of flying in an aeroplane (twin propeller, naturally) for the first time. In a little black-and-white photograph taken with Rosemary's Brownie box camera, Hilary and

I stand stiffly but smiling in our school uniforms in front of it. Of course, the Channel Islands were not really abroad but Jersey felt like it to me. The food was excitingly different and there were French words all over the place.

The hotel was some way outside St. Helier, right on the beach. While I pottered about and explored the bushes along the seashore, Hilary swam; like Rosemary, she was a strong swimmer. I remember how one afternoon, after we returned from the beach and Hilary wanted to change out of her wet bathing costume, as a childish prank I closed the door of our bedroom but stayed in the room and hid out of view at the side of the wardrobe. A few seconds later I popped out and said 'Boo!', catching her undressed. She was absolutely furious – the only time I ever recall her being angry with me – but it was several years before I began to understand why.

It was probably that autumn that Hilary was sent off to boarding school in North Wales, while I remained alone with Harold and Rosemary at No. 35. In a portrait photograph taken of me in my school uniform at that time, my hair has been bleached almost blond by the sun. I am not wearing glasses and am squinting myopically at the photographer, trying to focus on the camera. There is something quizzical as well as reserved about my expression as if there is something I haven't quite grasped. I am certain now that this was the period when everything started to change.

Often in the morning, especially at weekends, Harold would open the door to the corridor that led to my bedroom. I would hear the bottom of the door scraping on the carpet and Harold would then stand in the corridor, out of sight, and shout 'Rise and shine!' I hated this interruption to sleep or to an early morning doze, but I knew he would keep on standing there until he heard the noise of my getting out of bed. Satisfied, he would then leave, pulling the door shut behind him.

But one morning, he did not shout 'Rise and shine!' or remain standing at the top of the three stairs leading down into the room. He came in and sat down on the side of my bed, which woke me. I was lying on my back as he put his hand under the bedclothes and down the front of my pink and green striped Vyella pyjamas. I did not comprehend what was going on, but I knew I did not like it.

13

Perhaps if I shut my eyes it will stop.

* * *

One day, not long afterwards, while I was rummaging around looking for something to play with in one of the big wooden drawers of the workbench in the garage, which contained a First World War bayonet and other such oddities, as well as garden tools and cans of oil, Harold came up to me and gave me a brand new cricket ball, blood red and shiny with strange little bumps on it. It was surprisingly heavy for its size. I mumbled thanks and he went away, but I wondered what on earth I was meant to do with it. I did not have a bat and had no idea how to play cricket anyway, so I put it away in a drawer in the workbench. More importantly, I had not made close friends with any of the boys in Chatsworth Road who might know how to play cricket, though actually they spent most of their time running round the fields on the opposite side of the road waving wooden sticks that were imaginary rifles, killing make-believe Germans, or throwing stones at frogs by the side of the stream. With the exception of one lad called Peter who lived opposite, they tended to avoid me, that specky four eyes who was adopted from God knows where, and I did not particularly want to mix with them either. Way over the other side of those fields there was an estate of council houses, but I was forbidden by Rosemary from going there or having anything to do with children from the estate. They obviously had some contagious disease, so I kept well away.

Every so often, this quarantine mechanism intended to keep me apart from undesirable company broke down when gypsies came to camp on the fields, at a spot where an ack-ack unit had been located during the War. The sheds or Nissan huts or whatever had been there had long gone, but there were still brick foundations in the fields and you had to be careful not to fall down the entrance to underground shelters. The gypsies would arrive in their shabby metal caravans and soon would be knocking on the back door, trying to sell wooden pegs or begging for water. 'Don't give them any,' Harold growled, 'or else we'll never get rid of them.' Some of the boys looked pretty grubby but also rather wild and wonderful and I wondered what it would be like to stow away in one of their tatty caravans and take up a life on the road. But each time, after a few days – and presumably under pressure from the Eccles town council and the police – they disappeared just as suddenly as they had arrived.

'Better check in the garage to see if anything has been stolen,' Harold said after one such departure. Everything seemed in its place, but when I looked in the workbench drawers some weeks later, I noticed that the cricket ball had gone. I do not think it was the gypsies that took it, but Harold.

* * *

When he sits on the bed, I can't move, as my limbs are trapped under the bedclothes. But that does not stop him slipping his hand inside. It's like a spider that has plump pink fingers instead of legs – one wearing a gold signet ring – crawling slowly towards me. It's warm yet somehow it is cold at the same time. Sometimes I pretend it isn't happening, but I've also learnt how to block it out. I shut my eyes and soon all feeling goes from my legs and from my middle. Then I slowly leave my body, seeping out through the top of my head, hovering somewhere near the ceiling. On bright sunny mornings I can even go out through the window-panes and fly across the garden, then over the fields, riding on one of the soft white clouds. I'm so far out there sometimes I don't notice he has stopped, or even left the room, then silently I return back across the garden and through the window, then into the top of my head and down through my body, and gradually the feeling comes back to my legs.

I cannot make any sense of it all. But I feel so ashamed, and nobody must know this is happening.

* * *

Sometimes on afternoons during the summer holidays Rosemary took Hilary and me to Sunlight House in Manchester, where there was an indoor swimming pool. It had wonderful tile-lined cavities like half-submerged caves that you could swim in and out of like a fish. While Rosemary and Hilary were clocking up their lengths in the lanes of the main pool, I was whisking around this watery playground, imagining I was a dolphin in the Blue Grotto in Capri, which I had heard mentioned on the BBC. I was not really sure where Capri was, or indeed what the Blue Grotto looked like, and the tiles at Sunlight House were more green than blue, but that did not shatter the illusion. I happily stayed in the water for hours until my skin went all wrinkly and stank of chlorine. After drying off in one of the wooden cubicles I looked forward to a plate of beans on toast in the café located on the balcony that overlooked the pool, the amplified shouts and screams of other swimmers ricocheting off the ceiling. The waitress always gave me a cheery smile as she carefully placed the thick green china plate on the table.

We were never allowed to swim after this tea, because as Rosemary explained, if you swim less than an hour after eating anything, you die.

* * *

It has often been said that the British middle class discovered television in 1953, when they bought sets to watch Queen Elizabeth's coronation, but the Fryer household must have acquired theirs later as I distinctly remember it arriving: a large, double-doored contraption that looked more like a cocktail cabinet when its doors were closed. When it broke down – which happened quite often – an engineer had to come round to unscrew the back and then adjust or replace the disconcertingly large glass valves inside. He would then sit on the floor, twiddling knobs and cursing, while he tried to make the dizzy-making black-and-white test-card get into focus. There were just two TV channels – both black-and-white, of course: the BBC and Granada, the latter being the independent channel covering the North West of England that had only started broadcasting in 1956. Staples of children's television in those days were Andy Pandy, on Watch with Mother, and Bill and Ben the Flowerpot Men; I could not relate to Andy Pandy, despite his striped pyjamas not dissimilar from mine, though secretly I longed for a teddy bear just like his. However, I do remember imitating the voice

16

of the flower that would greet Bill and Ben with a high-pitched cry: 'Weeeeeeeed!'

Every summer, during the Wimbledon tennis championships, the television in the lounge became Rosemary's altar before which she would sit transfixed, her armchair barely six feet from the screen. At the windows the curtains were drawn, and she had placed a small, folding white tray-table over the half closed doors of the TV set, to screen out any remaining light, so she could get a really clear picture. Match after match she watched, immobile, silent, and woe betide anyone who disturbed her. The women's singles attracted her deepest devotion and one year when rain stopped play she declared that she had been invited to go to compete at Wimbledon herself but her parents had prevented her. But I suspected that was just another of her fantasies.

* * *

One of the few times I remember Rosemary going to the cinema in my early years was when she took me to see The Wizard of Oz. She had originally seen it when it came out in 1939 and decided it was a suitable film for me to get my first taste of the pictures when it was re-released in the mid-1950s. Unfortunately, I was too young and sensitive or too insecure to appreciate it; when Dorothy's house was whisked up into the sky by a whirlwind I screamed and continued screaming until Rosemary reluctantly dragged me out of the cinema and headed back home, grumbling all the way. From now on there would be no trips to the cinema with her; it would have to be a diet of old black-and-white Hollywood movies on the TV instead.

* * *

I could tell which day of the week it was at home by the food on the table at lunch, which in the North of England is often called dinner and is traditionally the main meal of the day. Typically, Saturday was a roast joint: beef, pork or lamb (my favourite); Sunday was the same joint, cold; Monday was shepherd's pie or Lancashire

17

hotpot, made from the remains of the joint; Tuesday was chicken; Wednesday, lamb chops; Thursday, pork sausages. Friday was fillets of plaice, fried in bread crumbs. And then the cycle started again, with the constant rhythm and inevitability of a mantra. Green vegetables, boiled in water laced with bicarbonate of soda until all the taste had gone out of them, were the usual accompaniment, along with potatoes, roast, new or mashed. Only water was served with the meal, until the Corona van started to do a weekly round of Ellesmere Park and dandelion and burdock became an alternative for me. The dessert was almost always 'TF': tinned fruit, though that was sometimes whipped with fresh cream into a delicious mousse. Lunch was always served at precisely one o'clock, as the pips for the one o'clock news (or The World at One, from 1965) sounded on the BBC Home Service and the voices of presenters and news-readers precluded all conversation. Tea was similarly on the table at exactly 6pm. Along with tea, at that meal there would be cold meats, a pork pie or crumbly Cheshire cheese, with salad or the remains of Tuesday's chicken in a creamy cold sauce, along with a loaf of Hovis and soft, round, white, flavourless barm cakes. There was usually a home-made chocolate or coffee cake on the go as well. Rosemary was a very good cook within her limited repertoire, though she claimed that at the time of her marriage she had been unable to boil an egg, as she had been brought up in a house with a live-in maid.

Rosemary's insistence on exact mealtimes she put down to her experience working in hospitals, but as I got older I grew to realise that they were her attempt to anchor herself in reality, on which she had an increasingly tenuous hold. She would sit for hours in the kitchen, drinking Nescafé stirred into a 50:50 mixture of boiled milk and water and smoking her Players cigarettes, chatting to the daily – Mrs Warburton or her successor Mrs Haigh – or just staring out of the window into the front garden. Her elder sister had been institutionalised after she and her family had returned from Germany and Harold was worried Rosemary would end up the same way. He told me once that they had adopted another child before the War, but Rosemary had not been able to cope and they had sent it back. But maybe that was just another of his lies.

18

The third drawer down in the painted wooden kitchen unit next to the sink, underneath the window through which Rosemary stared, contained shoe-cleaning equipment: polishes, brushes and dusters, all clearly marked to show which were for brown shoes and which were for black, which was for putting on and which for polishing off. The drawers were deep and surprisingly heavy and often jammed when one tried to pull them out. Harold had two favourite pairs of shoes, one black, the other brown, and he would corner me in the kitchen, take his shoes off and tell me to clean them. 'You should be proud to clean your father's shoes!' he would say when he sensed me recoil. But I wasn't proud. I felt humiliated.

And you're not my father.

* * *

I must have skipped a year at Branwood House, having accelerated academically once I could read what was on the blackboard, because I was only nine when I joined Mr Firth's top form. All my teachers up until then had been women, and the lessons Mr Firth gave were quite unlike any I had had before. There was a mixture of English and maths and some very basic French, but the most exciting subject was History, which really ought to have been called current affairs, the way Mr Firth taught it. There was a large map of the world pinned on one wall with the territories of the British Empire all coloured salmon pink, but as Mr Firth explained some of the colonies were now being given independence. He was not sure that was necessarily a good thing, or whether Africa in particular was ready, but he was proud of the dignified way Britain had handed over power in the Gold Coast, as Ghana had been known – such a contrast with the utter hash the French were making in Vietnam, not to mention Algeria! I suspect the tumble of names and facts that came out in these lessons left some of my classmates confused, but they entranced me. I followed avidly as Mr Firth pointed at the places he was talking about on the map with a wooden stick. Back home I would look the places up in the 1937 edition of the Encyclopaedia Britannica, whose 24 volumes almost filled a glass-fronted bookcase in the lounge. Harold had given the set to Rosemary as a first wedding anniversary present, though I never saw either of them consulting it. Volume 24 was the Atlas and Index, and even if half the maps were outdated, the frontiers and even the names of many places changed, it fired my imagination. I would lie under the dining room table (a favourite sanctuary from the oppressiveness of the rest of the house), savouring each page, running my finger along roads and railway lines that I was sure one day I would travel.

One particular lesson Mr Firth gave stays fresh in my mind to this day. The subject was China, and the point of his stick flew rapidly back and forth between the Chinese mainland and the island of Taiwan. The wicked Communists had seized control of China in 1949, Mr Firth recounted with passion, but Chiang Kai-Shek and his nationalists had regrouped on the lovely island previously known as Formosa and would return to mainland China victoriously any day. Perhaps hankering back to his period of national service, Mr Firth became particularly animated at this prospect and I was caught up by his enthusiasm, though maybe not in the way he imagined. I had no emotive feelings about Reds under the Bed or Chairman Mao – about which Harold would also rant from time to time – but China was instantly a magic name for me, a wondrous future destination. It might be half way round the world, but I would have to go there, to get away completely from No. 35 and Chatsworth Road, from Eccles and Manchester.

I must, I can and I shall.

* * *

The thing I hate most of all is when he catches me about to go into the toilet that is situated next to my bedroom door and he follows me in. He shuts the door behind us and gives a weird grin then he undoes the buttons of his fly and pulls out his big, raging red-helmeted thing, which bears little resemblance to what I have got between my legs. He plays with his thing and when he has had enough he pees and leaves. I am stood rigid, speechless and unable to urinate until he is well out of the way.

20

*If I sense he is around when I want to go to the loo, I hide behind
the bedroom door, and more than once I have wet myself there.*

* * *

Fryer's of Eccles dominated one side of Church Street, which was
the town's thriving main shopping street when I was a child, busy
with cars and delivery vans. The street ran down from the railway
station to the market, past the parish church, several pubs and the
Westminster Bank. One could see how Fryer's department store had
grown from its humble origins, as it had gradually taken over more
of the buildings along one side of the street. Even where some of the
original shops, like Hulbert's the jewellers, remained at ground floor
level, Fryer's had acquired the upper storey and knocked archways
through the walls, which meant that the furniture department on the
first floor resembled a series of individual rooms in a private house,
stuffed full of tree piece suites and the trademark reproduction pieces
Harold loved. However, his special domain was the carpet
department, which shared the ground floor with drapery and
chinaware. I was not permitted to roll around on the carpets that were
stacked in large piles, though that was very tempting. Besides, I
preferred the offices upstairs, where the women who worked there
allowed me to feed envelopes through the franking machine. Inside
the envelopes were the monthly statements for all the customers who
bought their household goods on hire purchase – a majority, it would
appear, from the mountains of mail that left the building, though
Harold warned me and Hilary that when we were older we must
never buy things on tick, as that was how people got into debt and
debt was an unspeakable catastrophe.

* * *

On Saturdays or during school holidays when the weather was
fine I sometimes used to walk down to Eccles, just to get out of the
house. I would wander round the market at the bottom of Church
Street, where I was not supposed to go, and listen to the traders
shouting their wares, or else go into the big Co-op store, which I was

21

amazed to learn was not owned by a family but somehow by the people who shopped there. The Co-op gave customers a little book and then when the people bought things they got stamps to stick in the book and somehow that meant they got money back later. The customers at the Co-op were a different sort of people from the ones I saw in Fryer's and Harold was angry when I once told him I had been there.

Sometimes I would call in at Bradburn's, the bakers in Church Street, which claimed (not entirely truthfully, I later discovered) to be the original makers of Eccles Cakes. These hand-made delicacies were smaller in circumference than the factory-produced version common today, but plumper and much tastier. The buttery pastry was flaky and stuffed with a mixture of currants, mixed citrus peel, nutmeg and sugar. They were best eaten hot and I would sometimes use my pocket money to buy some and then warm them up in the Aga back at No. 35, though Rosemary would chide me for ruining my appetite.

After my walk round Eccles town centre I would go to Fryer's in the hope of getting a lift home in the car, but if Harold was busy serving customers I would have to keep out of the way. There was a pillar between the downstairs part of the furniture department and the carpets section behind which I used to hide; from that vantage point I could still see what was going on in the carpet department. Harold at work was a completely different person from the one I saw at home, where he was grumpy and demanding, his flabby white face in an almost permanent scowl, or when he was in the car swearing at all the other drivers, cursing them as 'stupid buggers'. Here for a few moments on the shop floor at Fryer's I saw a different man, a Harold as presumably most other people saw him: smiling, solicitous, deferential yet expansive. He was charm itself, putting into practice the maxim that the customer is always right and must be treated with deference. But that was not the man I knew.

On a couple of occasions, when a boy of around my age was in the store with his parents, I saw Harold slip the kid sixpence. Once a father noticed and I thought he was going to object, but then he said to his boy, 'Thank the nice man for that, Robert.'

I feel a burning inside me and I don't understand: why does he give money to boys he doesn't know?

* * *

I was growing increasingly confused about the nature of the relationship between Harold and me as it seemed nothing like the inter-action between normal fathers and sons. Apart from the episodes of enforced intimacy he largely ignored me, even avoided me. I envied the children I saw walking in the streets with their fathers and mothers; in the Fryer household that never happened. Harold went everywhere by car, usually alone. Rosemary said he was nervous of showing affection because Hilary when an infant had once poked him in the eye when he sat her on his lap, but there was something more profoundly psychological about his inability to relate to children like a normal father. Yet suddenly he would spring surprises on me without warning, like the cricket ball.

One afternoon, he told me to get in the car, but he would not tell me where we were going, just that he wanted to show me something. We drove for some time until we got to the gates of a large, modern building with lots of windows which at first I thought was a hospital. In fact it was a Barnardo's Home for orphans and children who had been taken into care. We were shown round by one of the care staff, and we saw groups of children having their tea at formica-topped tables: spam sandwiches and sliced white bread with jam or something of the kind. The children stopped eating for a moment to stare at us as we passed through and I in turn stared at the floor, embarrassed. Had Harold or Fryer's made a donation to the home, I wondered? Why had he brought me to Barnado's? Surely he wasn't going to leave me there?

'You see how lucky you are,' was all he said as we got back into the car and then silently drove back to Eccles.

I was really shaken by the prospect of ending up in such a place, and made myself swear inwardly that I must not say anything to anyone about any of the things that were happening at home, or else that would be my fate.

23

* * *

Not long after this, probably during the Easter school holidays, I was sent away for the first time. I don't remember getting any warning that this was going to happen, but Harold announced one day that he was taking me to stay on a farm as this would be 'good for me'. He had spent some time working on a farm as a boy, during the First World War, in which he was too young to serve as a soldier but there was a shortage of labour on the land as most of the young men had gone off to fight. I was pleased to get away from Eccles for a while and quite excited about being with animals, with which I felt a greater affinity than with most of the humans around me, so I was quite disappointed when, after a long drive through Cheshire and into North Wales, the car drew up outside a small stone cottage with rows of vegetables growing in the front garden. Mr and Mrs Williams were Welsh-speakers, but she seemed friendly enough as she took me up to a small bedroom at the front of the house, whose widow looked out over the lane. The ceiling was low and although I was still a boy I felt it was pressing down on me. There was a china bowl standing on a chest of drawers and a big jug full of water for washing oneself sitting inside it. Through the window I watched Harold drive away; then I was called downstairs to have some tea.

Mr and Mrs Williams did not appear to have any children; certainly there were none living in the house. He was taciturn in the extreme and seemed to resent speaking English on the few occasions he made a remark in my direction whereas she burbled on, asking me what I liked to eat and how much milk I wanted in my tea. This struck me as strange, as at No. 35 I just ate or drank whatever was put before me; any failure to eat everything up as quickly as Harold and Rosemary did would be met with an admonishment from Rosemary that I must think of the starving children in China and clean my plate. The logic of that failed me, even as a child, but I had long since realised that it was best to keep my head down and do what I was told.

I realise now that the Williamses in North Wales must have taken me in as a paying guest – the first of many such arrangements – though I have no idea how Harold knew or chose them. There was no

24

television in the house but my hosts sat listening to the wireless after tea and I went back upstairs to read a book I had brought from home. I was woken early the following morning by Mrs Williams; her husband had already finished his breakfast when I came down and was waiting impatiently by the back door. I had not realised the previous evening, but behind the cottage there was a line of wooden hen-houses, all painted black; the Williamses' small-holding was essentially a chicken farm and indeed in the hedge at the front by the side of the road there was a hand-painted sign: Free Range Eggs. I was puzzled why Mr Williams would want to give his eggs away for free, but followed him silently into the hen-houses as he showed me how to remove the eggs carefully from the nesting boxes and lay them gently in a metal pail. The hens clucked disapprovingly, but did not seem particularly fussed about having their produce taken away and were soon back out in the field happily pecking away. 'Tomorrow you can collect the eggs,' Mr Williams informed me.

Meanwhile, there was nothing to do. Mrs Williams did not want any help in the kitchen and there did not seem to be any books in the house apart from a big black Bible. I went for a walk in the lane, but soon the pollen from the wild flowers and the freshly mown grass in the fields got up my nose and my eyes started itching. By the time I got back to the cottage, I was sneezing noisily and my eyes were streaming. I was wearily used to hay fever every summer at home, but this was more extreme. By the time I went to bed, I was coughing repeatedly and I could hardly breathe. I barely slept that night and was drowsy the following morning, when I was called down to breakfast. I had to wash my eyes with a flannel doused in water to get them open as the lids were stuck together. Mrs Williams clucked sympathetically while Mr Williams glared, but after breakfast I was handed the metal pail and sent out to the hen-houses.

Very slowly I went from one to the next, carefully extracting the eggs and ignoring the squawks of the hens that seemed much louder than when I had gone round with Mr Williams the previous morning. There did not appear to be quite as many eggs in the pail, either, so when I had finished in the last hen-house I went back to the first and started all over again. Only a very few eggs had appeared in the time since my first round and most of the hens had gone outside, but the total haul looked respectable by the end of my second round so I thought Mr Williams would be pleased. I did a third round of the hen-houses just to check there were not any last minute additions, but as I walked towards the back door or the cottage Mr Williams stormed out, swearing in Welsh. The reason I knew it was swearing was because every so often he used the English word 'bloody'.

Mrs Williams came out after him and tried to calm him and took the pail of eggs from my outstretched hand, but her husband was still ranting, gesticulating around the field. Only then did I notice that the chickens were no longer contentedly pecking on the ground, but were running hither and thither, some trying to scramble out through the hedge, frightened by my repeated intrusions into the hen-houses. Mrs Williams shooed me up to my room while she dealt with her husband. My hay fever had by now started up again and soon I was wheezing asthmatically.

Mr Williams must have phoned Harold, straight away, because within a few hours his car was outside the gate and I was being ushered out. I did not hear whatever words were exchanged with the Williamses, but maybe because I was sneezing so much, Harold drove back to Manchester in stony silence. I knew I was in disgrace, but I was glad to be getting away from the countryside that made me so ill and where life seemed so boring. But I was not looking forward to returning to Chatsworth Road, where I knew Harold's visitations would start again once his temper had cooled. I closed my eyes and wished I could just disappear.

* * *

I would love to have an older brother. There is enough room in the bedroom over the garage for another bed and we would be able to talk about everything. I could ask him about things I don't understand and tell him about all the places I dream about. I might even show him the stories I write, which I hide at the back of a drawer in one of the chests in the bedroom, underneath two rubber hot water bottles.

It would not matter that I don't really have any friends if I had a brother. We could play together, as long as he was not too much

26

older, of course. In my imagination he is about two or three years older and blond and does not wear glasses. And he is good at sport.

If I had an older brother, perhaps Harold would not come into my room to fiddle with me anymore. Well, he wouldn't be able to, would he?

* * *

The world of which Mr Firth's lessons had made me aware was now being brought into sharper black-and-white focus through the pages of a weekly publication, The Children's Newspaper, which got delivered to the house, along with Harold's Daily Telegraph and Rosemary's Manchester Guardian. The paper's motto, 'The Story of the World Today for the Men and Women of Tomorrow', thrilled me and I was soon building on my knowledge of far-flung places and their geography and history. I think it must have been from there that I learned about World Refugee Year. There had been a huge migration of people in Europe after the Second World War, not least of ethnic Germans pushed out of central and eastern Europe; nearly fifteen years after the end of the War there were still many tens of thousands of displaced people living in refugee camps on the continent, so the United Nations designated 1959-1960 as World Refugee Year, with the stated aim of emptying the camps once and for all. Dozens of countries issued commemorative postage stamps to mark the year, which excited me as a novice philatelist, buying for a few pence exotic postage stamps sent 'on approval' through the post by an agency based somewhere in the Midlands. But I was determined to do something about the problem of refugees myself; there were people who were hungry or without a proper home and one could not just ignore their plight, I argued.

At one local primary school, children had volunteered to go without their biscuits for one day a week, donating the money saved to the World Refugee Year Appeal, but that struck me as being very tame. Instead I resolved to organise a garden party of the kind some churches in the area put on in the summer, only mine would be in the Easter holiday 1960. I went from house to house in Ellesmere Park, knocking on doors and asking for donations of anything that could be

27

put on sale, from second hand clothes and costume jewellery to children's toys and books. Almost everyone had something to donate, even the Bishop of Middleton and his wife, who lived in a large house opposite the Lodge at the other end of Chatsworth Road. Rosemary, Hilary, Auntie Ruth and various young neighbours and Hilary's friends were commandeered to man the stalls which filled the ground floor of the house and part of the garden. Mercifully on the day the weather was fine, the neighbours came to look and buy and the event raised £11 (the equivalent of nearly £230 in 2016). The local newspaper, the Eccles Journal, wrote an article about it, but far from being pleased I was furious, as the journalist wrote that I was 10-years-old, whereas I was still only nine. At that age, such things matter.

* * *

Maybe it was because of the article in the newspaper that I was invited to the birthday party of a boy I hardly knew, the son of the landlord of a big red-brick pub in Eccles town centre. These were not the sort of people that Harold and Rosemary considered respectable – neither of them would have dreamt of setting foot in any of the numerous pubs in the area – but I was pleased to be asked, as I did not get many such invitations. The problem was that it was a fancy dress party and there were no fancy dress costumes at No. 35 and Rosemary was not a woman who could rustle one up. So I had to go as I was. When I arrived at the pub, the landlord's wife took pity on me and led me upstairs to their flat and rummaged around in an old trunk, from which she produced a Scottish kilt, but unfortunately it was far too big, so I had to stay as I was. The culmination of the afternoon was a fancy dress parade, in which each child had to announce what he or she was meant to be as they walked past the judge (the pub landlord). Rather than just sit on the side-lines, I took my turn and announced myself proudly as 'an English boy', which provoked howls of derision. 'You're just stupid!' the birthday boy shouted to laughter from his mates, so I slipped away and slunk back home.

* * *

Once a year, throughout my childhood, a Miss Johns would appear at our house. She was middle-aged (at least that is how she appeared to me), trim, with her hair pinned up, and dressed in a sort of business uniform, like an Avon lady – the housewives who made a little money for themselves by selling beauty products door-to-door. But Miss Johns dealt not in beauty products but in babies, as I learned when I was old enough to understand such things. I don't think she was a social worker from the council, but rather a representative from the agency through which my adoption had been arranged, between Harold and Rosemary on the one hand and my birth mother on the other. Every year, in summer time, Miss Johns would appear – probably on a Sunday afternoon, when Harold would be home from work but back from golf – to ask them if everything was going alright. I would be sent out into the garden to play, but I used to sit on the step of the porch by the front door, straining to try to hear anything they were saying. But of course I could hear nothing. And after an hour or so, Miss Johns would leave, giving me a little nod and a smile, and I would be told I could come back in.

And me? Don't I get a chance to say whether everything is going alright or not?

* * *

I took the 11+ exam that divided English schoolchildren into the sheep and the goats (grammar school entrants and those destined for the secondary modern) more or less on my 10th birthday. I enjoyed exams in those days and was still good at them, which meant that I assumed I would pass the 11+ and go on to Eccles Grammar School, which was also within walking distance of No. 35. However, Harold and Rosemary had other ideas. He had left school at 14, though after the First World War he attended night classes, whereas Rosemary had gone to boarding school. Most of the Fryer cousins had also gone to boarding schools, as Hilary did, and in fact my name had been put down for Oundle in Northamptonshire. But Harold and Rosemary had decided that I would continue living at home for

29

whatever reason (with hindsight, I have my suspicions in his case) and insisted that I should try to get into one of the more competitive grammar schools in the Manchester area instead. I remember going to Bolton Grammar School to sit an exam there, successfully, as it happens, but that place was turned down when I passed the exam for Manchester Grammar school (MGS). Founded in 1515 as a free boys grammar school, located adjacent to the church that would become Manchester's Anglican Cathedral, it outgrew its original premises and in 1931 moved to a greenfield site in the suburb of Fallowfield, just south of Didsbury. Now an independent day school, in 1960 MGS was still a direct grant school, which meant that it took in pupils entirely on merit from all over Greater Manchester, irrespective of their parents' financial position. A central government grant paid for most of the cost, and the top-up fees were scaled in proportion to the parents' income, with those from the poorest backgrounds paying nothing. This system meant that Harold had to pay the maximum – a fact he liked to rub in with me, as if somehow it was my fault. Manchester Grammar was by far the largest of the direct grant schools, with over 1,000 pupils (all boys), and had an unparalleled reputation, not least for getting its sixth formers into Oxbridge colleges.

Far from being on my doorstep, MGS necessitated a long journey through Salford into the centre of Manchester and out again past the university to Fallowfield. On my first day, in September 1960, Rosemary accompanied me on the bus from the bottom of Chatsworth Road to Deansgate in Manchester, from where we then had to walk to the side of the Victorian architect Alfred Waterhouse's magnificent Neo-Gothic Town Hall in Albert Square to catch another bus to the school. This was the first and only time for many years that Rosemary used buses. The journey took almost exactly an hour in total, and for the next nine years that was to be my daily term-time commute. The distance was not huge in miles but the traffic was often bad, especially in winter or when it was raining hard. The first bus came from Eccles town centre and after picking me up on the corner of Chatsworth Road, opposite the Lodge, wound its way through the council estate where I had been forbidden to go, then round to Hope Hospital and past Millionaire's Row, a series of enormous mansions that had previously been the homes of Salford's industrial grandees but which by this time had fallen into multi-occupancy or ruin. Before long, almost all of them would be demolished. There were still tramlines running along the main road, though the trams had long since gone, and the buses rattled and shuddered as they ran over them. On the way into Salford city centre, there was mile upon mile of terraces of back-to-back brick houses, the models for Coronation Street, the Granada Television soap opera that began that very year of 1960.

The remaining civic buildings and churches in central Salford – including the Catholic Cathedral – were black with soot and therefore looked depressing but there was one church that made me smile with its hoarding outside, like an advertising billboard, proclaiming 'God Washes Whitest'. This was the Salford that 18-year-old Shelagh Delaney had captured in her play A Taste of Honey, which premiered at the Theatre Royal Stratford East in London in May 1958. I had read about that, and I'm pretty sure I saw the documentary Ken Russell made about life in Salford that was shown on the BBC in September 1960, in which Shelagh Delaney recalled her childhood there. Harold thoroughly disapproved of this 'muck', as he called modern drama and its subject matter. What he read about kitchen sink dramatists like John Osborne in the Daily Telegraph just reinforced his view that the country was going to the dogs. He took a pretty dim view of actors, too. In order to survive while learning his thespian craft, the young Albert Finney, who hailed from Pendleton, had worked briefly as a warehouseman at Fryer's before Harold gave him the sack. 'Useless bugger. Head in the clouds,' was Harold's verdict. Harold never, ever, went to the theatre, except to see Ken Dodd perform at the Palace Theatre in Manchester, when he would happily sit for hours roaring with delight at Dodd's recounting silly tales of diddy-men while waving his tickle-stick. Rosemary preferred the television and thought Doddy went on far too long, which he did.

My journey to school took me past the Granada TV studios and sometimes on the way home I would get off the bus and hang around outside, to see if I could spot one of the stars. I bought a little autograph book with pastel-coloured pages and was thrilled when

31

Violet Carson – Ena Sharples in Coronation Street – was the first person to stop and sign and have a chat, though I almost did not recognise her without her hairnet. She seemed like someone who would make a wonderful granny, though I was surprised that she did not speak with the broad Lancashire accent that she had in the show. My own accent had already been neutered by an elocution teacher, to whom I was sent for an hour every week during my last year at primary school. His idea of correct pronunciation was based on BBC radio announcers; while not as clipped and haughty as the voices of the commentators on Pathé newsreels shown in cinemas, the BBC announcers' enunciation of the Queen's English had a precision that made many Mancunians laugh. It certainly did not help to make me popular among my peers when my own vocal chords had been trained to speak that way. The odd thing was that Harold never tried to alter his own Northern tones and even if I was dissuaded from mixing with the offspring of the working class, he said he was proud of his father's humble origins. As a symbol of his supposedly being a man of the people, in winter Harold always wore a cloth cap outside, even when he was driving around in his Daimler.

* * *

To a 10-year-old coming from Branwood House, Manchester Grammar was dauntingly huge. I had been kitted out at Kendal Milne's department store on Deansgate, which I suspect was the monopoly supplier of the school's uniform: coarse grey flannel shorts (for the junior boys), long socks, navy blue blazer and a cap which had a little metal owl sewn onto it. Though the school had an imposing front entrance with a drive leading from high metal gates through the sports fields to the arched entry to the main quadrangle, like most of the boys I went in through the much more modest back gate, where the school porter, Wilf, in his three-quarter length brown linen overcoat, was a reassuring, lingering presence. One then walked past the tuck shop and through some cloisters into the school proper. There were rows and rows of coat hooks in cages along the corridor outside the main assembly hall, which could accommodate about 800 lads of varying ages as well as the masters in their academic gowns for the daily assembly; the numerous Jewish boys had their own gathering elsewhere. In the first week, all the new boys had to go for a medical examination; after a quick look in my hair to make sure I didn't have nits – which some of the new cohort from poorer homes did – and a listen to my chest with a stethoscope (no asthmatic wheezing, now the hay fever season was well and truly over), the doctor told me to pull down my shorts so he could have a feel to see if my testicles had dropped.

So it isn't only Harold that does this. Yet it doesn't feel quite the same.

* * *

In those days, when boys entered the first form at MGS, they had to opt either for the modern or classical stream – or else their parents did on their behalf. I certainly don't remember Harold or Rosemary ever asking me which one I would prefer. The difference was that on the modern side, pupils began with French and Latin but later had to study German as well, whereas on the classical side, Latin was emphasized, with an option to choose ancient Greek later. I can only assume it was my adoptive parents' own inability at modern languages, or else a lingering dislike of the Germans, that made them opt on my behalf for the Classics. So I was allocated to 1gamma, the lowest stream on the classical side. This would prove to be a disastrous choice that would adversely affect my school performance for the next several years. Although I was aware that one had to have Latin 'O' level to go on to Oxford or Cambridge University, as a 10-year-old I had absolutely no feeling for the Ancient world and found the Latin lessons mystifying. The elderly Latin Master tried to explain everything in terms of a railway system – 'cuius junction' still sticks in my mind – but I didn't have the foggiest idea what he was talking about and simply was not interested. Mathematics bored me too and even English was uninspiring, as it was all about grammar, rather than literature. Literature did rouse my passion, but out of school time. I had taken advantage of the large array of books assembled for the garden party the previous Easter to lay the foundations of a respectable little library in my bedroom at No. 35.

33

When I got home from school, I would go up there to read until I was called for tea at 6pm and as soon as I was allowed to get up from the dining table, would be back among my books upstairs, as Harold and Rosemary settled down to watch the television or had a couple of their friends round from Worsley Golf Club for a game of bridge.

At Manchester Grammar I found myself unable to concentrate on the classes. My mind was elsewhere, yet nowhere. I would run the point of a pencil along the grooves in the wooden desk top, back and forth, silently, until I went into a sort of trance that was only broken by the shrill ringing of the bell at the end of the lesson. I was oblivious to the boys around me and just fitted in automatically to the routine of the timetable, queuing for a little bottle of milk at break-time, mechanically eating the dreary food that was dished out by the dinner-ladies at lunch in the refectory. The end of the school day saw scores of boys racing for the special buses that were lined up on the main road near the school's back gate, but I did not run nor join in their ragging once on board. In Manchester, between buses, I would often linger in the streets, looking in shop windows or wandering round Kendal Milne's, putting off going home.

I dreaded the weekly gym classes at school, which were run by a martinet who would have been better suited to the army than to MGS. I would get half way up the wall-bars and then freeze, unable to move, while the red-faced gym master shouted at me until eventually someone helped me come back down. When I tried a running somersault I just ended up as a crumpled heap on the mat. There was no way I could propel myself across the wooden horse. It was if I could not control my body and all the time my mind was asking *what is the point of all this?* In contrast I loved the swimming periods. The school had a large indoor pool and the water was warm. We boys would hang our clothes up on pegs in the changing room and then dive in naked. Many of my classmates had to be taught to swim from scratch, as they had never been to a swimming baths, but I was in my element. I was bottom of the class in almost every academic subject, but in the swimming pool I was as adept and confident as a fish.

* * *

34

Sometimes I lie in bed wondering when he will come in next. It's impossible to predict, as I guess he just seizes the chance when Rosemary is out of the house. Perhaps if I tell myself it isn't happening then the nausea I feel when he is touching me will go away. Perhaps if I tell myself it isn't happening then it can't be my fault, as I increasingly feel it must be. Perhaps if I tell myself it isn't happening then one day I'll be able to persuade myself that it never happened at all.

* * *

In the Easter holidays of 1961, Harold and Rosemary sent me to school camp at Borrowdale in the Lake District. We boys slept in large tents by the side of a stream and had to cook our own food over brushwood fires. The morning porridge stuck to the pans and was hard to clean off in the cold running water of the stream. I was the youngest boy there, still quite skinny and wearing thick glasses that made me look pretty weedy. One evening, after the masters had in principle seen us off to bed I was dragged from my sleeping bag by some older boys in my tent, stripped naked and tied to one of the tent-poles. They made fun of my hairless body and undeveloped genitals and then started talking about sex – the first time I ever recall the subject being mentioned. I knew women had babies but I had no idea how they were made; Rosemary had once flippantly remarked that one found them under gooseberry bushes, causing me to cast a suspicious eye at the garden of No. 35. But now as I stood there in the tent in Borrowdale, sniffling and trying to keep back the tears, my mind was going into overdrive with the older boys talking about girls and the way women had to use bloody 'jam rags' (sanitary towels) to wipe themselves and other such things that left me reeling. 'I bet you can't even get it up!' one prefect jeered, as he slapped my willy.

With my mind in turmoil I could not appreciate the beauty of Derwentwater and the surrounding countryside of the Lake District and I hated walking in the rain. The master in charge kept us to a strict routine: 50 minutes walking, then 10 minutes rest, as if we were soldiers on a long campaign march. On the last day, in Keswick, I bought a tiny, kitsch leather-bound concertina of photographs of the Lake District for Rosemary with my remaining half-crown, though I knew Harold would be angry that I had bought nothing for him, as indeed he was. But before that confession, when the coach had brought us boys back to Manchester and he came to pick me up in the car, I blurted out as soon as I had got in what had happened in the tent and how much I had hated it. If I expected sympathy, I did not get it. I had never seen him so angry, yet not at what the boys had done but seemingly at me. He told me to shut up. 'And don't say a word about this to your mother,' he said. 'Not a word. Do you understand?' At the time, I thought he wanted to prevent her being upset, but now I realise it was because he was worried I might also tell her about what he had been doing to me as well.

What suddenly became clear to me, as it had never been before, was that Harold's fiddling with me had something to do with sex. I was still unsure what it all meant but suddenly I knew that it was not just unpleasant but dirty and wrong. My dislike for him was turning into a burning yet unvoiced loathing, but I also hated myself and I began to blame myself for what was happening. I was unclean and there seemed to be nothing I could do about it.

* * *

The Irish doctor, Dr Moroney, and his wife who lived next door at No. 33 Chatsworth Road with their two daughters, Moira and Anne, were Catholics, which is why Harold and Rosemary would have nothing to do with them. While I was still at Branwood House, I used to go round to see Moira, who had a wind-up gramophone handed down though the family on which we used to play 78rpm records of 1940s dance music in the garden in the summer. It must have been on Moira's gramophone, with its imposing golden horn, that I first heard Paul Robeson sing and I marvelled that there was a different sort of culture, not just American but African-American, of which I had not been aware.

Moira's younger sister Anne was blind and lived largely in an imaginary world of her own making. For hours she would position herself on a grassy knoll by the side of the family's garage – just over the hedge from our side garden – and jig around, not exactly dancing, but moving around on the spot, waving her arms up and down, and talking to her imaginary friends.

'That girl's not all there,' Rosemary would say, as we caught sight of Anne out of one of the side windows of our lounge. 'Jonathan, stop staring!'

'Why? She can't see me!' I would protest.

'That's not the point,' Rosemary would say, as if that settled everything.

But when she had left the lounge, to have a cigarette and a milky coffee in the kitchen, I would look out again at Anne, bobbing up and down, with a beatific smile on her face.

'Don't worry, Anne,' I say to her telepathically. 'I can hear them too.'

* * *

My schoolwork in the summer term of 1961 was so bad that the school called Harold and Rosemary in to discuss the situation. The form master felt it could not just be the hay fever – though that did add to a growing problem of insomnia, which left me drowsy during the day, made worse by the antihistamine tablets I was taking. My form master was concerned that I seemed to have made no friends in the class and appeared totally disengaged. Was there anything the matter? 'Of course, I told him there was nothing the matter,' Rosemary informed me when she got home. 'I told him I was expelled from my school,' she added triumphantly, 'and I've turned out alright, haven't I!'

MGS accordingly did not expel me nor recommend that I be taken away. Instead, it was agreed that the problem was probably that I had just been too young when I started at the school, and that if I did the first year again – this time in 1alpha, not 1gamma – the matter might be resolved.

To get my mind off school and my troubled wakening thoughts about sex, I organised another garden party at No. 35, in the week of my 11th birthday. Hilary, who must have been home on half term holiday from Howell's School in Denbigh in North Wales, dealt with soft drinks with her best friend Jennifer, while Peter from over the road manned the book table, Moira from No. 33 was on the white elephant stall, and the Bishop of Middleton's daughter (another Jennifer) ran the bagatelle. I sold toys and tried to keep an eye on everything. It was a bigger event than that of the year before, but the weather was not so good, so it was not as busy as I had hoped. Still, it made £14 (over £288 in 2016's money). This I decided would be divided between Dr Barnardo's (my visit there was still etched in my mind) and the Women's Voluntary Service, who put their share towards the cost of an outing to Lymm for a party of old age pensioners who were beneficiaries of their Meals-on-wheels service. While I could not concentrate on classes at school, keeping busy organising things like the garden party, or cataloguing my ever-expanding bedroom library on little cards like I had seen used at Eccles public library, helped my mind stop thinking about other things.

* * *

Harold and Rosemary's Silver Wedding anniversary that summer was a big affair, by their standards. Caterers had been brought in to do the food and all morning vans arrived bringing bunches of flowers from relatives and their friends from the Golf Club to the extent that there were soon no more vases or pots to put them in. To Hilary's and my acute embarrassment, Mrs Moroney from No. 33 leant over the hedge and handed over a particularly beautiful bouquet wrapped in cellophane. She and her husband had deliberately not been invited and had to listen to the many guests enjoying their cocktails and buffet lunch in the garden on a gloriously sunny day.

Harold had made it clear that he expected Hilary and me to do something special to mark the wedding anniversary, given all that they had done for us as adoptive parents, so the two of us decided to pool our pocket money savings and to take them to dinner at a smart hotel in Chester. The menu was unlike anything I had ever seen before, and I was particularly tempted by the idea of potted shrimps as a starter. Unfortunately they must have been off – or maybe there was something already wrong with me – as very shortly after finishing the first course I felt distinctly sick. Rosemary took me out into the street while I waited for the nausea to pass but I knew I would not be able to eat anything more. Disappointed at the way the evening had from my point of view been ruined I exclaimed, 'Oh! What a wicked waste!', which Rosemary thought was hysterically funny. This was a story she repeated with gusto for years to come.

* * *

It was also in the summer of 1961 that I started over-eating. I had got used to Rosemary serving me a small tin of Heinz spaghetti or baked beans with mini-chipolatas every weekday morning before sending me off to school but now I was snacking heavily between meals. I would raid the biscuit tin, or cut myself a slice of bread which I then spread with butter and sugar or Heinz salad cream; this latter sickly open sandwich for some reason I cannot now remember I called a Romeo and Juliet. When I started back at MGS in the autumn I would often go to a pie shop in the centre of Manchester on my way home and scoff the pie before I got on the next bus home. At night before I went to bed, I would have a bowl of Sugar Puffs with milk along with my Horlicks or cocoa. At weekends I would sometimes buy Eccles cakes as before, but now I could not wait to get to the house to heat them up, but instead sat among the graves around Eccles Parish Church, looking at the names on the gravestones, wondering if any of them were members of my real family. Even if it was raining, I would sit down among the headstones and eat the Eccles cakes cold, the raindrops that were trickling down my face making crumbs of pastry stick to my chin. Then one day workmen came and flattened the gravestones and turned them into paving stones and I never sat by the church again

Rosemary saw nothing unusual in such an accelerated appetite in a growing boy and it is true that I was getting taller quickly, as well as noticeably fatter. By the end of the year I was easily the chubbiest boy in my class and from my observations in the swimming pool, there was only one lad in our year who was bigger than me, a short Jewish boy who was clinically obese. I did not like being fat and it was the cause for rude comments and a limited amount of bullying from some of my classmates, who on one occasion stuffed me bottom downwards into a metal waste-paper bin and threatened to kick me down the stairs.

However, unlike in my first year, where I had got to know none of my fellow pupils, in 1alpha I found a friend, John Jenkins, a rather timid lad who was short and skinny and a bit of a misfit like me. We sat next to each other in some of the classes, and as he was extremely ticklish, I enjoyed tickling him sometimes so that he would disappear under the desk, which caused the rather jolly form master, Mr Corbett, to ask, 'Where's Jenkins? I'm sure he was here earlier.' I think he was well aware of our game.

John lived in Swinton and had a pet guinea pig, which I found enchanting on the few occasions I went to visit him at home. The animal made a noise like 'wink wink' when stroked, which led to me renaming Jenkins Winkins. By coincidence he was friendly with Peter who lived opposite me in Chatsworth Road, so sometimes he used to get the bus home to Eccles with me. We told each other funny stories or made 'winking' noises at each other. The other passengers must have thought us very silly. However, there was a favourite conductress on the route, a jolly German woman, who used to jangle her leather satchel full of pennies as she came round with her ticket machine, and she was always ready with a joke for us boys. She was the first foreign person I had ever spoken with and she was so nice that it made me wonder what the War against the Germans had all been about.

I guess it was in the summer of 1962 that I invited John to come and stay with us at the cottage that Harold and Rosemary had taken to renting every August, right on the beach at Porthdinllaen on the Llyn peninsula in Gwynned, North Wales. In fact, all the properties in Porthdinllaen were on the beach, as there was no road to the little fishing village (a panorama of which would later become an iconic image for the National Trust's advertising campaigns), just a dirt track down the hill from a small cark park at the far end of the local golf course, which was Harold's main motivation for choosing the place. Several of his chums from Worsley Golf Club also rented properties in Porthdinllaen for the summer. To get to the village you had to have a key to the gate at the entrance to the golf course and drive slowly along the unmade road in the hope that no-one would slice a ball through your windscreen.

The terraced cottage was in a tiny row rather grandiosely named Whitehall and had no mod cons, though downstairs there were gas lights with incandescent mantles which ran off big calor gas bottles, as did the oven. Upstairs one had to use candles. There was no running water; that had to be fetched in tall plastic containers by rowing boat from a standpipe in the next bay. The toilet was an Elsan in a shed at the side of the cottage. Every day except Sundays, Evans the Milk would come over from the nearby town of Merthyr Tydfil with waxed cartons of fresh milk that often went off before the day was over, as there was no fridge or indeed electricity. When he had finished his milk round this elderly fellow in a black cloth cap would transform himself into Evans the Can, to refresh the chemicals in the Elsan and clean the toilet shed. Goodness knows what modern health and safety officials would have made of all that.

The downstairs of the cottage was essentially a kitchen plus a big living room, with a dining table and a few chairs in the latter. Every time anyone came in from the beach the floor got covered in sand and if one wasn't careful that got into the food as well. At home in Chatsworth Road each member of the family had their own weekly bath night, for which water was heated in an electric immersion heater which was located in a cupboard in the bathroom. But in the cottage in Porthdinllaen the only option for bathing was a tin bath in which you had to sit in the living room, showering yourself sparingly from a jug. Upstairs there were three bedrooms, the third only accessible through one of the others as it was built over an arch at the beginning of Whitehall. I thought it was exciting sleeping there at first, but it got tedious when grown-ups in the next room protested at being woken by one creeping through with a candle if one needed to

41

use the loo. I suppose John Jenkins and I must have shared a bed there; friends often shared beds in those days. What I do remember is one awful mealtime when he was with us. Rosemary had failed to buy enough butter on her recent shopping trip into Merthyr Tydfil, so there was only a tiny amount left in the butter dish on the table. John helped himself to a normal amount, at which Harold shouted at the top of his voice, 'Put that back!' Anyone would have thought John had committed some terrible crime and he was clearly shaken. I was embarrassed and angry for him but bit my tongue.

At other times, those summer breaks in Porthdinllaen during my early teenage years were a welcome release from the oppressiveness of Eccles. On the hottest days, with my skin plastered with vinegar (which served as a sort of protective sun lotion), I would sit on the beach with my back leaning against the wall below the Ty Coch pub, helping a woman called Nora do the Daily Telegraph crossword. The weather was usually good and often I could get away by myself for most of the day, rowing the boat that went with the cottage round to the next bay to fetch water, or walking in the other direction along the narrow cliff path lined with wild flowers that linked the village to Lifeboat Bay, where I would sit by the side of the deserted lifeboat shelter and look out across the sea. Ireland must be somewhere out there, I reasoned, even though I could not see it. On other occasions I would go out with the local fishermen to help bring up the lobster pots. It seemed so strange that the lobsters would be so stupid as to walk into the wire cages on the seabed, from which they had no escape; surely they saw others trapped in that way? Some of the lobsters were really large and the fishermen would bring them ashore and then knock on the doors of the cottages that were holiday lets, to sell them, holding the struggling creatures out in their leathery hands, the lobsters' claws fastened shut with rubber bands. Rosemary would sometimes buy one and put it in the plastic washing-up bowl, half-filled with water, where it would scrabble around until the large pan of water on the gas cooker came to the boil. Then the lobster would be plunged head first into the boiling water. Rosemary insisted it could not feel anything and would die instantly, but I hated to watch, though I was fascinated how quickly it turned from black to pink. It was probably when I refused to eat any of the lobster on one occasion that Harold shouted at me that I did not know how lucky I was and that he was fed up of me being so ungrateful. Unusually, I snapped back at him, at which he retorted that he was sorry Rosemary and he had ever adopted me. This was one of the few times we were ever in total agreement.

* * *

The hay fever and associated asthma had become so debilitating that I was sent for a day of Bencard tests at one of their allergy units. In those days this involved injecting subcutaneously tiny amounts of different irritants – grass pollen, cat fur, house dust and so on – into one's lower arms to see how seriously allergic to each thing one was. My arms erupted into a series of red welts, showing that I was allergic to practically everything. Accordingly, for the next several years, during the winter months, I used to have to go to the surgery of the family doctor, Dr Price, twice a week for injections in my upper arms before I went to school. The hope was that this would reduce the symptoms when summer came, but in fact the injections seemed to have little effect, other than making my upper arms very sore. Antihistamine tablets brought some relief but made me so drowsy that I sometimes dozed off in class. On occasions the asthma was so severe that I could not go to school at all. At least twice I was sent away to Wales, not to a farm this time but to a small guesthouse in Rhyl on the coast, accompanied by my godmother Auntie Ruth, in the belief that the bracing sea air would do me good. Being by the seaside during the day did help, but I still struggled for breath in bed at night and Rhyl had little to offer beyond the funfair, which palled after a while.

I spent a lot of time in North Wales in the early 1960s, not just because of the annual holidays in Porthdinllaen and the trips to Rhyll. Several times a year Harold, Rosemary and I went over to Denbigh to take Hilary out on a day's exeat from school. The large grounds of Howell's with its open-air swimming pool were impressive but I was more struck by seeing a real live black person for the first time, a student of the school who was a daughter of King Freddie, more correctly Mutesa II, the Kabaka of Buganda in

Uganda, which gained independence from Britain in 1962. At home, I had often played as a small child with one of Hilary's cast-off dolls, a black plastic girl the size of a human baby but totally naked; but King Freddie's daughter was dressed in school uniform just like the other girls. The exeats with Hilary usually involved driving around a lot of countryside, the inside of the car filled with the smoke from Rosemary's cigarettes, before we had lunch at some hotel. The place I liked best was the Grand Hotel in Llandudno, which was a vast Victorian pile at the end of the promenade, with long corridors of empty function rooms through which I used to run. My godparents Jack and Joan had built themselves a very modern house with huge picture windows on the Great Orme at Llandudno and moved there from Eccles, so on at least one occasion I went to stay with them there as well. One of the exeats with Hilary I remember vividly was in the autumn of 1962, when we had left the grownups and were listening to a transistor radio and heard the Beatles' *Love Me Do* for the first time. It sounds corny to say it now, but like millions of other youngsters we were both bowled over by this fresh sound from the four lads from Liverpool. However, when Harold heard a song of theirs for the first time he said, 'Turn off that noise!'

* * *

I was feeling trapped in No. 35 and increasingly miserable at school. There seemed to be no escape as I shuttled daily back and forth between the two. Yet I felt if only I could contact my real mother maybe everything would get better. I was bursting to pour out my unhappiness to someone, but did not feel I could burden Hilary with it all or my friend John Jenkins. It never occurred to me to try to talk to one of the masters at school, and in those days they were not trained to look for signs of sexual abuse or other domestic problems among their pupils. Instead, I thought a doctor might be the best person to turn to. It did not seem wise to broach the subject with the family doctor, Dr Price, as he knew Harold and Rosemary too well, so instead I went to see another doctor, who lived in Chatsworth Road, at his home. I started to explain that I really wanted to know who my original parents were, at which point he interrupted me

44

angrily saying that was a wicked thing to think about, after all Harold and Rosemary had been doing for me. How could I be so ungrateful? There was that word again: ungrateful.

Don't you want to know why I want to know my real parents? Can't you see there's something wrong?

The doctor ushered me out, telling me to push thoughts about my background out of my head. I went into the fields instead of heading straight back to No. 35 and sat down, pulling blades of grass from the ground, rubbing the sharp edge along one of my fingers until it bled. There was clearly no point trying to talk to any grown-ups. They belonged to a different species.

* * *

I have a recurring dream, in which I go up the three stairs leading out of my bedroom and along the corridor that leads to the main part of the house, but when I open the door I am in a different place. It is a huge Victorian building, more like an abandoned palace than a house, and yet I know that I live there and that I am happy there. I move from one vast room to another, each devoid of furniture except for floor-to-ceiling bookshelves full of dusty tomes. I want to show this all to someone but nobody is there and as I run faster and faster through the open doorways looking for somebody I start to panic.

Then I wake and I am engulfed in waves of disappointment. I am back in the bedroom over the garage at No. 35 and when I climb the three stairs and go to the door to try to find the entrance to the magical palace, it isn't there.

* * *

Although presumably much of what I studied in 1alpha at MGS must have been similar to what I was exposed to in 1gamma the year before it did not strike me as particularly familiar and I did just as dismally as before, bumping along as no. 30, 31 or 32 out of 32 in the class for most subjects. However, my interest in English literature prompted me to join the Drama Society and to my surprise I was picked to play a role in the First Form play, a one-acter set in a courtroom in which my character was one of the star witnesses. I suspect I was chosen mainly because of my portly figure, which gave me a certain spurious gravitas. I certainly enjoyed the rehearsals, which took place on the stage of the school's fine theatre, with its curious smell that was a mixture of actors' make-up and dust. Sometimes I would sit in the stalls and watch the term's main play being rehearsed, principally because one of our neighbours in Ellesmere Park, Robert Powell, was playing the lead and even as a schoolboy he was a highly accomplished actor whom it was a joy to observe. Six years older than me, Robert out of school hours was already doing professional roles at the Piccadilly Studios for *Children's Hour* on the BBC, as well as weekend plays for the BBC in Leeds, with Albert Bradley. I watched him with awe in plays both ancient and modern, in parts both young and old, male and female. It was clear that he had a great acting career ahead of him, yet after MGS he went not to drama school but to the Royal College of Advanced Technology in Salford before doing an external London University law degree at the Manchester School of Commerce. That was the sort of career path middle class families like ours expected, not something frivolous and insecure in the Arts. Serious professions were also what the intellectual sausage machine that was MGS in the 1960s was finely geared to. Captains of industry were what the school was good at producing, not people in the creative sector (though that later changed). I was perversely pleased to learn that the 18th Century self-styled English Opium-Eater, Thomas De Quincey, had only lasted a little over 18 months at the school before running away.

A few weeks before the play I had been cast in was due to be performed, I went on a school trip to London – the first time I had set foot in the capital. We were housed in some sort of Territorial Army or similar camp in Chigwell in Essex, where the ablution blocks were separate from the dormitories, necessitating a quick sprint in pyjamas between the two first thing in the morning. The washrooms stank of disinfectant. Every day we were driven by coach into London through slow-moving traffic before starting the day's itinerary. I do not recall much about the trip as on the day we went to Madame

Tussaud's I collapsed in the waxwork museum's Chamber of Horrors. Once the staff had established that I was really ill and not just over-emotional, an ambulance was called for and I was taken off to St. Thomas's Hospital by the Thames. I was given a bed in the men's ward, but not allowed to fraternise as it turned out I had mumps. When I had been brought in, the Sister had asked me if I knew anyone in London and I told her that the only introduction I had been given by Harold was to Sir Ralph Perring, who that year was Lord Mayor of London. I don't think she believed me, but it was true; Harold and he had worked together in the National Association of Furniture Makers and Perrings the furnishers was a familiar name in many of England's high streets. I wrote to Sir Ralph from my hospital bed and although he understandably did not come to see me, he did send a get well card. Only when the hospital was sure I was no longer infectious did they send me back to Manchester. In the meantime, at school another boy had slipped into my role in the First Form one-acter and my acting career thus came to an ignominious end before it had even begun.

* * *

Although the mumps were indeed cured, my general health was deteriorating fast. In 1962 few people believed that children could suffer from depression or other forms of mental illness, but half a century later it is clear to me that that is what was developing in reaction to my hatred of Harold and his fumblings, of No. 35 and of school. I was sleeping too long, over-eating and failing to connect with most of the people around me. Then the panic attacks and fits began. Typically, I would be sitting in class, not following what was going on, when my heart suddenly started beating faster and my breathing speeded up. I was by that stage unable to speak, but by the time I was taken down to lie on a camp bed in the sick bay by the side of the gym I was often convulsing violently. In the worst instances, I then briefly blacked out, before coming round with a terrible headache. Only then did my power of speech return. The dreaded gym master, or whoever was around, would run off for the school doctor or someone would say, 'We should send you home.'

47

'No, I don't want to go home,' I would manage to reply and I would lie there for half an hour or so, until my body was behaving itself again, and catch up with my timetable of lessons or, if it was late in the afternoon, slowly make my way back to Eccles.

Why don't you ever ask why I don't want to go home?

Of course the school told Harold and Rosemary what had happened the first time it occurred, and the Fryers took me round to see Dr Price. He was non-plussed, as there seemed to be nothing fundamentally wrong with me as far as he could see, but he referred me to a consultant. Rosemary went with me and therefore heard at first hand the tentative diagnosis that it might be *petit mal*, linked to a form of childhood absence epilepsy. Some of the symptoms did indeed seem to fit the bill. But whereas a typical childhood absence seizure will last for between five to 20 seconds, during which the child is unresponsive to anything around it, in my cases the 'absences' were much longer and followed violent convulsions that in turn followed hyper-ventilation. Though the specialist was unsure about his diagnosis I was put on some medication that was meant to stop these attacks happening. It did not, but in the meantime it made me feel like a zombie.

* * *

Around this time, Harold pulled another of his surprises. One afternoon when I got home from school he announced that the two of us would not be eating at home that evening but instead would drive over to Halifax to visit the owner of a carpet factory which was one of Fryer's suppliers. I assumed we would be going to the factory, though I was puzzled why it should be open so late, but instead when we got to Halifax we drove up to an imposing Yorkshire stone house. This was where the factory owner lived; a jovial man of around Harold's age. With him was a much younger man, who obviously lived there too. I wondered if he was a son or a nephew, but now realise he must have been our host's live-in partner. There were just the four of us at dinner, at which the adults had wine – something that never, ever happened at No. 35. I do not remember any of the conversation, but I was impressed by the beauty of the house, its furnishings and the paintings – original oils, unlike the hideous reproduction of a country cottage by a stream that hung over the settee in the lounge at No. 35. After dinner Harold and I drove back to Eccles in silence, as my mind tried to come to terms with the question *what was that all about?*

* * *

It was also around this time, when I was 12 or 13, that Harold stopped coming into my bedroom, just as suddenly as he had started to do so about five years earlier. I had refused to go with him into the toilet anymore and he must have sensed my growing hostility and defiance. Besides, I was no longer a cute little boy, but an overweight adolescent with a growing complex of physical and mental health problems. Sometimes I would lie in bed at night hoping I would not wake up in the morning. By now I had a bicycle and once I cycled several miles to a footbridge over the main Manchester to Liverpool railway line where I thought how easy it would be to jump. But then I realised that if I did jump this would not be in the hope of killing myself but rather to land in one of the goods wagons passing underneath so that I would be taken away, far away.

A good part of my anxiety was by now not focussed so much on Harold as on myself and my own first stirrings of sexual awareness. When I lay face down on the carpet in the lounge and moved slowly back and forth I felt a pleasurable sensation in my groin. In bed I found myself touching myself and when I did that I did not vacate my body, as used to happen when Harold fiddled with me. I was starting to get sensations that I had never felt before and did not know even existed. There had been no sex education at either Branwood House or MGS (nor would there ever be) and when I had my first erection I went into a blind panic. To make things worse, this happened at a time when I had entered a period of religious fervour, which meant that I was overwhelmed with guilt.

Although Harold and Rosemary had no time for organised religion, they had sent me to Sunday school at the Congregational Church in Eccles for a while, mainly, I suspect, to get me out of the

49

house on the one day that Harold did not go to work. At Sunday school, under the gaze of a blond, blue-eyed Jesus with long flowing hair and a beard, I learnt some Bible stories and a few of the basic tenets of Christianity. But I stopped going to Sunday school after I went to MGS and thought no more of religion until my guilt over my sexual awakening sent me in search of forgiveness in the established Church. Though churches were somewhere Harold and Rosemary went to just for weddings, christenings and funerals, I started cycling to Eccles Parish Church every Sunday morning for the 8am service. Sometimes there was no-one else there when I arrived, and the elderly vicar would shuffle around in the vestry, peeping out every few moments, until he was sure that some other people had arrived and that the service could therefore go ahead. The New English Bible (New Testament) had been published in 1961 and I bought a copy from a Christian bookshop in Manchester, its meaning resonating more clearly with me than the King James's authorised version used in the parish church.

* * *

At Easter 1962, Harold and Rosemary took Hilary on a package holiday to Cascais in Portugal. I was farmed out to a family at the other end of Chatsworth Road who had a son of about my age. I imagine this was as a paying guest once again, as we did not know the family very well. I enjoyed this break living in a normal household and one weekend they drove over to the coast to visit one of their in-laws, Jimmy Armfield, who was a footballer who played for Blackpool and was Captain of the England football team at the time. He lived in a very modest house; the beautiful game had not yet made multi-millionaires of the best players. I lingered in the hall on arrival at the Armfields' home, as I was shy about meeting him, but my host family laughed and ushered me in. I was speechless, not just because he was a well-known name but because he was so extraordinarily fit, unlike any man I had seen in real life before, as well as relaxed and smiling. He told me about matches he had played in an international tournament in Brazil and although I had not the

slightest interest in football and the forthcoming World Cup, or indeed in any sport, I was smitten by him.
I wish you were my uncle. No, I wish you were my dad.

* * *

Hilary returned from Portugal deeply bronzed and it suddenly struck me that she had become a beautiful young woman. On her bath nights when she was on holiday from Howell's she spent longer in the bathroom than any of the rest of us and she started to build a small wardrobe of smart clothes. She even did a spot of modelling at Kendal Milne's once, though I think that was for a lark rather than with any serious intent of pursuing a modelling career. A girl in Chatsworth Road had just got a job as an air hostess, which was considered by Harold and his golf club circle to be the most glamorous work opportunity possible for a young woman, but that was not something that appealed to Hilary. Her social set, when she was home from school and later from physical training college, was based on the tennis club, where she was understandably popular. It was not a world I would ever be part of, but I realised how proud I was of her. And although I never breathed a word to her about what had gone on at No. 35 while she was away until after Harold's funeral over 20 years later, we were close and wrote regularly. For her birthday one May, I bought her a pair of green satin high-heeled shoes because I wanted her to look her best.

* * *

You never hit me, but sometimes I wish that you had. Then there would be bruises to show, whereas now there is nothing visible that reflects the pain and the anxiety inside me that won't go away.
Sometimes I try to provoke you. Once I blew a toy trumpet in your face and then ran half-way up the stairs. 'Come here, you little bugger!' you shouted, but you stayed standing in the hall and did not try to come after me. I gave another short blast on the trumpet and then went into my room, pulling the door shut behind me.

51

The summer of 1963 was a period of growing anguish about school. If I moved on to the third form on the classical side I would have to study Greek, which was unthinkable. I still had not got my head round elementary Latin, which at least was written in recognisable letters. But it was impossible to transfer at this late stage to the modern side instead, as my French was very weak and I had no German. So the only alternative was to move in the autumn to a class called S3L – the 'S' representing science and the 'L' Latin. As my lack of interest in physics and chemistry was even more profound than my dislike for the Classics, this was a gloomy prospect. The end of term report from my form master that summer had a certain tone of exasperation, declaring that it was not clear what I was interested in, if anything, but whatever I was going on to do in life it obviously must not involve languages.

The great irony was that it was that very summer when I suddenly realised the point of learning French. It is hard to imagine just how monocultural and monolingual Manchester was half a century ago, or at least those parts with which I came into contact. Apart from the German bus conductress and the family dentist, Dr Schindler, who had come to England before the War as a Jewish refugee from Nazi Germany, I had not spoken to any continental Europeans, let alone anyone from Africa or Asia. But in the summer of 1963 I went on a week-long school trip to Paris, Versailles and Fontainebleau – proudly clutching my first, stiff dark blue passport – which fundamentally changed my perceptions. It was a mixed-aged group of boys, accompanied by a couple of masters, and I was astonished and impressed that one of the older boys was able to converse freely with people in shops and in the street. I decided on the spot that I would make sure that one day I would be able to do that too.

We were all put up in a rather shabby one-star hotel called the Hotel de Nice in the rue de Rivoli on the right bank of the Seine, which was not then as smart an area as it is today. Indeed, when I looked out of the window of the bedroom I shared with another boy, I was dismayed to see men sleeping in the doorways of neighbouring buildings. One of the older boys in our group sneaked into a shop and bought a small bottle of calvados, which he hid up the chimney of his room. When he brought it out late at night he and his closest chums quickly got drunk and several were violently sick. I was too young to be included in this bacchanalia, and anyway would have been much too nervous to try.

We had our meals in a self-service restaurant in St.-Germain des Prés, which was remarkably cheap and really rather good. I had never seen anything like the array of dishes on offer. At school the grey and beige, tasteless food, half covered by a skin of congealing gravy, was plonked down in front of us by the dinner ladies, with no question of any choice unless an individual had special dietary requirements. The Paris restaurant was also convenient to many of the historic sites and as I tagged along with the older boy whose language skills had impressed me I began to appreciate the attractions of a culture that lived largely outside, not indoors, in warm weather. For the Parisians this involved sitting on terraces at the Café de Flore or the Deux Magots, or strolling along the boulevards, or browsing in the *bouquinistes* on the banks of the Seine, where it was still possible to buy 19th century engravings and illustrations from fashion magazines from La Belle Époque for the equivalent of a few pence. Many of the buildings were in a poor state of repair and looked as if they had not been painted since before the War, but there was an appealing raffishness about the city and I was enchanted by the funny old single-decker buses which had a platform all the way round at the back where passengers stood to watch the world go by or to be able to jump off from the gap at the back whenever they wanted. It was also in Paris that I saw street-walkers for the first time, not having got to Soho on my ill-fated trip to London. My older companion explained that these working girls were paid for sex, but I still had no clue what a man and a woman did together to make babies. Was kissing enough?

* * *

Back in Manchester, the first time I had a wet dream I was mortified. I do not remember which images provoked this, but I set about cleaning the sticky mess on the sheets with a handkerchief in the hope that no-one would notice. Did this mean I was going to become like Harold, I wondered? I prayed to God to forgive me and swore that I would never allow myself to do it again. I dismantled the green trestle table on which my small model railway, a hamster's cage and a budgerigar's cage had sat at various times over the previous few years and converted one of the folding trestle legs into a makeshift altar. I draped a bed sheet over that as well as an exquisite piece of 19th century Japanese embroidery which a friendly couple who lived at the other end of Puddly Lane had given to me. I found an antique candlestick at the bottom of a drawer and went to a Christian shop in central Manchester to buy a small self-standing wooden cross with a metal body of Christ nailed to it so the space near the end of my bed had been transformed into a kind of little chapel. Before this altar I knelt at night to pray, sometimes for an end to world poverty and war, but mainly for the state of my soul. The fact that I was so miserable had to be some form of punishment for being such a wicked child and for doing wicked things, I reasoned. If I did not repent now I would surely pay for it later.

I had picked up some Christian pamphlets at Eccles Parish Church, including one from the Church Missionary Society which talked about missionary work on behalf of the Church in South India. That sounded immensely appealing and the illustrations of tropical communities full of smiling, happy people ready to discover Jesus was seductive. However, I was still only 13 and the possibility of joining an organisation such as the CMS was only a far-off dream. Nonetheless I decided to go to seek some advice. As the Bishop of Middleton lived down the road and I had already had contact with him and his wife because of the charity garden parties, I boldly walked up to their back door and was let in to the kitchen by the wife. The bishop was at home, and to his great credit agreed to see me when I told his wife why I had come. So I was shown through the hall into his huge, book-lined study.

Ted Wickham (as he preferred to be called) was a small man who looked quite tiny in this imposing room, but he was welcoming and curious. Although only a suffragan bishop (not that I really understood the difference), he had acquired a degree of national fame, and in some quarters notoriety, with the publication in 1957 of his book *Church and People in an Industrial City*. For nine years he had been canon residentiary at Sheffield Cathedral before being appointed Bishop of Middleton in 1959. He believed that the Church needed to adapt to the modernised world and in particular learn how to communicate its message in an understandable way to industrial workers. Unsurprisingly, he was therefore a socialist, and as such beyond the pale as far as Harold was concerned, though the Bishop's wife Helen was in the same Ellesmere Park women's discussion group as Rosemary until Rosemary stopped going. The bishop listened patiently as I shared my desire to become a Christian missionary in India but suggested first maybe I should get confirmed in the Church of England and study a little theology and then come back and see him again in a few years' time.

I felt deflated, but I saw his point and did duly sign up for weekly confirmation classes at Eccles Parish Church. These were run by the old vicar himself in his study in the vicarage. As I recall, there were only about five us who attended. Each week we discussed a passage from the Bible; just seven verses each time. We were told which seven verses these would be the week before and were encourage to think deeply about one verse each day. As someone who was by now reading an average of one book a day, mainly fiction, I found this concentration on such a short piece of text deeply frustrating and could not help myself racing on ahead. At each confirmation class the Vicar asked each of us in turn how many verses we had indeed read (some invariably confessed to none), and one week I declared proudly, '64!' I thought he would be pleased, but on the contrary he was visibly annoyed. 'Jonathan, I don't think you are taking this seriously!'

Oh, but I am, Vicar. You don't know how seriously. You don't know how much I need to be redeemed.

* * *

Though reading books had often been the way my mind escaped the confines of No. 35, I was finding it increasingly difficult to concentrate on the text before me, even adventure stories by John Buchan. I would finish a page and then realise that although my eyes had followed the words along each line they had not taken any of them in, which meant I had to read the same page two or three times and then often I would give up. Television was much less demanding and became a sort of sedative. I could watch it without thinking as the hours passed by until it was time to go to bed.

Accordingly, I was quite put out when shortly after tea on Friday 22nd November 1963 there was suddenly an interruption to the Granada TV programming for an announcement that the US President, John F. Kennedy, had been shot in Dallas, Texas. In fact, Granada was the first UK channel to carry the news, followed shortly afterwards by confirmation that the President was dead. The evening schedule of ITV programmes was cancelled and instead Granada broadcast solemn music played by the Hallé Orchestra. Of course I knew who Kennedy was and I had followed the Cuban missile crisis on the TV news the previous year. Yet I was so bound up in my own mental turmoil that I was unable to register the significance of the assassination, or even to feel any real surprise at his death. I turned over to the BBC, which was screening an episode of Here's Harry, a sitcom about an inept ditherer played by Harry Worth. It was not a programme I particularly enjoyed usually, except for the sequence during the end credits, where Harry stood by a reflective window of a shop in St. Ann's Square, Manchester, then raised one arm and a leg, creating the optical illusion that he was spread-eagled, like one of those toy figures on a stick whose legs and arms all went up when you pulled a string. I'd sometimes done the trick in that window in St. Ann's Square myself and it always made me laugh.

Harold came into the room at that moment and frowned. 'Turn off the television, now! President Kennedy has been shot! Show some respect!'

I switched the knob to off and shut the TV cabinet doors, then went upstairs to my room without saying a word. How can I show respect to someone I don't even know, I wondered, when I don't even respect the adults living in this house?

* * *

This was the period when Fryer's, the business, was at its zenith. A large extension was added at the back of the Church Street store, more than doubling the size of the carpet department. Smaller branches of the store were up and running in Bury, Bolton and Stockport and the youngest of the 13 Fryer siblings had opened an estate agent's in central Manchester. There was a small estate agents section on the first floor of the Eccles store too, next to a counter for the Burnley Building Society, where I opened an account. If I was going to go off to South India at some time in the future, I reckoned I had better start saving up some serious money. Our pocket money was not especially generous, but apart from the meat pies and the Eccles cakes I still bought on a regular basis I did not really have any outgoings. Rosemary gave me the bus fare and the one shilling and three pence (£1.91p at 2016 prices) for the daily school dinner ticket. Books I borrowed free from Eccles Public Library. Moreover, I was supplementing my pocket money with earnings from a paper round in Eccles town centre and occasional odd jobs. That included working on Saturdays at Fryer's carpet department, for which Harold paid me £1 a day (£19 in 2016 terms). I did not handle any of the big sales, which mainly involved fitted carpets, but there was a brisk trade in small rugs and mats, some of which were actually free samples from carpet manufacturers which customers were nonetheless happy to pay money for.

Sometimes an attractive woman in her mid-30s comes into the shop and looks around, trying not to draw attention to herself. 'Can I help you, Madam?' one of the sales-ladies from the china or drapery department will ask her after a while, as they have been trained to do in such circumstances. 'Oh no, just looking, thank you,' the woman says with a smile, before slowly leaving the store, her eyes still scanning left and right. That woman is my mother, and she is looking for me.

* * *

Although Harold was no longer coming into my room, there was silent open warfare between us over the dining table. I had to sit opposite him and just watching him eat made me want to vomit. So I

57

would fix my gaze over his head, focussing on the ornaments that sat on top of the sideboard behind him, mostly clunky glassware that must have come from Fryer's, though there was also an exquisite china figure of an old Russian man with an umbrella which had been part of the small trove of treasures that had come down from the white Russian refugees so many years before. But soon that figurine got moved up onto the top of the pelmet above the French windows, as Harold was worried someone might break it. No pictures were ever hung from the picture rail that ran round the rest of the dining room walls, but at Christmas time all the Christmas cards that Harold and Rosemary received would be stuck on top of it with Sellotape. They got scores of them, and in the last few days before Christmas there would be four or five postal deliveries a day as students, including Hilary, helped out at the Post Office. Various manufacturing firms which supplied Fryer's used to send gifts and samples to the house at Christmas as well; one company always sent a hamper of tinned and preserved foods. One year the hamper contained a bottle of wine, which Harold put away in a chest of drawers in one of the bedrooms. When I had to empty the house many years later, after both he and Rosemary had died, that bottle of wine was still there in the drawer.

Just as Fryer's the shop had been extended so No. 35 got refurbished as well at this point. The Aga in the kitchen and the coal-store by the back porch were both removed and central heating and an electric cooker were installed. Both the lounge and the dining room were extended back a short distance, swallowing up the previous veranda. A large car-port was built in front of the garage so there would be room for Rosemary to have her own car, an Austin Mini, which for some unknown reason she named Priscilla. These cars had first been made in 1959 but by 1963 they were almost symbolic of Britain's swinging Sixties, not that there was anything swinging about Rosemary.

The car port had a flat roof which I could climb onto from the window at the front end of my bedroom. From that vantage point I could see out over the fields on the other side of Chatsworth Road, which were gradually being tamed and would eventually be turned into school playing fields. I still used to go and play in those fields out of summer time, when the long grass no longer made me sneeze, and I could imagine I was a long way away. But one day Rosemary told me I must stay away from there for a while. Through the kitchen window I then saw that there were police cars outside and Bobbies in uniform were fanning out across the fields. It turned out that a man had assaulted a boy who had been playing in one of the tunnels under the old disused railway track and the boy's parents had called the police. They were treating the matter seriously as they were worried the man might strike again.

If I find that man before they do, maybe he will take me away with him, and I could get away from Eccles for ever. I wonder what he is like. Maybe he's a traveller, like those gypsies that used to come and stay in the fields when I was small. Or maybe someone who likes books and all the things I like? Oh no, maybe it's HIM!

* * *

Under the circumstances, it was unfortunate that Harold had meanwhile booked a two-week summer break for himself at the Hotel Atlas in Cala Mayor on the Spanish island of Mallorca and arranged for me to go with him, in principle to look after him in case he fell ill. He was already well into his 60s, though he looked even older, and his health was starting to fail, as each year he spent longer periods in bed coughing with bronchitis and wheezing with emphysema, doubtless made worse by Rosemary's smoking. She had moved out of the twin-bedded master bedroom that they had previously shared – the only one that had an electric fire, before the central heating was put in, and which now stank of Vick's VapoRub – and henceforth she spent increasing periods of time in her new bedroom alone. It was clear to me that their relationship had soured a little, though I did not know the reason why. One Saturday lunchtime, half way through the meal, Rosemary suddenly stood up, crying, and rushed out through the French windows into the garden. 'Go and see to your Mother!' Harold said. But instead I simply left the room, thinking that whatever the problem was it was something they had to sort out for themselves. It had nothing to do with me.

59

The Hotel Atlas in Mallorca was on a side street set back from the beach at Cala Mayor. There was a crazy golf course nearby, which I found more appealing than the real game on which Harold was so keen, and the roads were lined with flowering shrubs whose pale pink blossoms scented the air. The temperature was hotter than anything I had ever experienced but when I was not on the beach I was exploring the road that led to the capital, Palma. Harold and I shared a twin-bedded room, which meant that I hardly slept at night as he snored loudly and I resented being in such close proximity to him. Accordingly I tended to nap in the afternoon, often at the side of the swimming pool of the larger hotel next door, which we were allowed to use. Harold never went into the water as he could not swim.

One afternoon while I was dozing by the pool I suddenly heard Harold calling my name. When I had managed to put my glasses on, I saw that there was a little boy, several years younger than me, splashing around in the water, obviously in difficulty. Unfortunately, far from diving in to rescue him, as doubtless Harold expected, I froze on the spot. A second or two later a man did jump in and pull the spluttering child to safety. I watched as the boy's anxious family gathered round to reassure themselves he was OK. Then I realised Harold was standing over me.

'You're useless, bloody useless!' he said, then walked away.

While you are lying there asleep and snoring it would be so easy just to take a pillow and press it down over your head. You would probably feel nothing, not even realise what was happening. No-one would know until the chambermaid found your body in the morning and maybe the hotel would just think you had died in your sleep. I would be long gone, hiding somewhere in the middle of the island until I knew it was safe to appear, or maybe I would find work on a farm. But of course I could never kill you. I am incapable of doing such a thing. But every morning I wake up hoping I will find you dead.

* * *

My imagination did give me some moments of respite from the violent thoughts that had been generated by despair. Perhaps fantasy would be a more accurate word. There was a black-and-white American television series that was aired in Britain for several years in the mid-1960s called The Fugitive, starring David Janssen, which became more real to me than my surroundings back at No. 35. The story line was simple: a doctor, Richard Kimble, had been placed on death row, having wrongly been found guilty of murdering his wife. While he was being moved by rail from one jail to another, the train crashed and he was able to escape, and for the next four years or so in my mind I was on the run with him, trying to keep one step ahead of detective lieutenant Philip Gerard, whose mission was to capture us. Gerard was played by the actor Barry Morse, but in my mind's eye he was a younger version of Harold, doggedly pursuing Dr Kimble and me across the country. Dr Kimble had seen a one-armed man running away from the scene of his wife's murder and he believed that if only he could find that man he would be able to prove his innocence. This quest increasingly obsessed me.

Dr Richard Kimble (or in truth the actor David Janssen, with his swarthy, mixed Jewish-Irish heritage) was the most handsome man I had ever seen. I used to lie on the sofa in the lounge when the programme was on, just staring at him in wonder. Through the neck of his shirt, soaked in sweat, one could see the thick black hair of his manly chest. I imagined what it would be like when we were hiding in a barn, having once again given Lt Gerard the slip. After a simple supper of bread and cheese stolen from some farmer's kitchen we would lie down in the straw and I would fall asleep in his arms, protected from all the dangers of life by him.

One day my heart missed a beat when I saw in the Radio Times or some other such publication a competition in which the prize was to go to Hollywood for a tour of the film and TV studios finishing with dinner with David Janssen. I must have sat looking at the associated terms and conditions for half an hour. I was barred from entry because of my young age, and I imagine the competition was targeted at Janssen's millions of women fans rather than at boys, yet strangely I did not feel disappointed. It was not just that I knew I would not win, even if I had been able to enter the competition, but rather that I did not want to win. It was not David Janssen that I had fallen in love with, but Dr Richard Kimble. And for the rest of my teenage years, when I was lying in my bed in the room over the garage, unable to sleep and feeling even more depressed than usual, it was Dr Richard Kimble who came at night to comfort me.

* * *

While the house was being altered, the kitchen was out of action for several weeks, so Harold, Rosemary and I went to Worsley Golf Club every evening for supper. In principle that was not the only option; an Italian restaurant – the first of its kind in the town – had opened at the top end of Church Street in Eccles, near to the railway station, and Jimmy Armfield's relative with whom I had been briefly housed had caused great merriment among the staff there by ordering spaghetti and chips, as was reported in the local paper. But Harold did not like the sound of Italian food, so instead it was the Golf Club that we went to night after night, where he and Rosemary spent a lot of their time anyway. Although Harold had heavy work responsibilities as Joint Managing Director of Fryer's that did not stop him playing golf or spending hours in the large men-only snooker room, which reeked of pipe smoke and beer. Women were confined to a much smaller mixed bar – whose main attraction was one of Manchester's first one-armed bandit fruit machines – and the restaurant. So for several weeks, each evening instead of having tea at home we would have a drink in the mixed bar – gin-and-tonic for Harold, Amontillado sherry for Rosemary, Britvic tomato juice with Worcester sauce for me – and then go through to the dining room to eat. I think I had sole mornay almost every night.

* * *

At school, science proved to be even worse than I had feared. Physics was a mystery I was happy to leave unexplored, whereas chemistry offered little that interested me, apart from the aesthetic attraction of different types of litmus paper that changed colour when dipped into a test tube containing an acidic or alkaline solution. At my request, I had been given a 72-colour set of colouring pencils for my birthday, a sturdy cardboard box that opened out like an old-fashioned travelling trunk, with row upon row of every shade imaginable of the different colours of the rainbow. This box of pencils took up almost all the room in my fat leather briefcase, but I carried it around everywhere. In chemistry lessons, when everyone was meant to be drawing diagrammatic representations of experiments that were going on at the front of the class, I instead spent the time colouring various shapes and imaginary landscapes that I had drawn. At first the chemistry master used to get annoyed about this, but then he decided it was easier just to let me get on with it.

I was much more excited by the prospect of biology, as I had developed a deep interest in the natural world. I had successfully completed a number of the one shilling I-SPY colour books on categories such as birds, wildflowers, butterflies and moths, dutifully noting down each species that had been spotted before sending off to Big Chief I-SPY Arnold Cawthrow in London for a dyed bird's feather and a certificate; I would have had enough feathers to make an Indian head-dress had I known how, but instead they just languished in the bottom of the wardrobe until I decided I was too old for such childish things and threw them away.

In the meantime, I had set up the Beeley Ornithological Society, Beeley being the house name given to No. 35 by Harold and Rosemary in memory of the area in the Peak District of Derbyshire where they had done their courting in the mid-1930s. Goodness knows why I thought it necessary to start a new society for bird-watchers when so many existed already, but I put together a committee made up of various adult neighbours plus Auntie Ruth, and the man who had given me the Japanese silk hanging that was draped over my home-made altar by the side of my bed produced some original bird notelets for sale, to raise funds. I wrote to the naturalist Peter Scott (only son of Scott of the Antarctic), whom I had seen presenting the BBC's natural history series Look, asking him if he would be the Beeley Ornithological Society's patron, though when he replied remarkably promptly accepting the invitation I was disconcerted by a line in his letter in which he defended hunters for their role in conservation. To my young mind, with its black-and-white perceptions of such matters, hunters who shot birds and animals for 'sport' were evil, no two ways about it. The fact that Harold had a gun which he kept in a cupboard in the kitchen was another black mark against him, though he had not used it for years and eventually he got rid of it.

I decided the best way I could carry forward my new crusade to help birds and animals was to become a vet. Having recently joined the Central Library in Manchester, which was conveniently located on the walk between the two buses that I had to take to get home from MGS, I borrowed a weighty tome on farriery, to learn about the care of horses' hooves. Rather than just take notes from this, I decided I would make a copy that I would be able to keep forever. I had acquired a very heavy old manual typewriter that was being discarded from the offices at Fryer's and sitting with this at the desk in the dining room I started to type out the text of the book from the beginning. As I had not yet learned how to touch-type it took me several hours to type out the first few pages, at which point I lost heart and gave up.

At school, there was an even worse dampener on my ambition to become a vet. I had naively assumed that biology would be all about looking at pictures of plants, insects, birds and animals and admiring a few living examples but I had not been prepared for dissection. When in one class we boys were shown how to use a small electric charge to make a frog's leg twitch, so we could observe the muscle movement, I revolted. Vivisection and anything similar to it were things I was not prepared to do. The biology master, an avuncular figure who smoked a pipe, was intrigued by this sudden crisis of conscience and invited me to accompany him on a walk all round the school playing fields to try to persuade him why in future I should be excused from attending biology lessons. I obviously succeeded, as it was agreed that instead I would spend the time in the school library, reading. As I had already managed to get out of playing sport because of summer hay fever and year-round myopia, instead spending the sports lessons reading in the library, I was managing rapidly to broaden my knowledge of English literature, history and geography in the school library's large and tranquil series of rooms filled with books but usually empty of boys.

* * *

At No. 35, I tried to avoid being in the same room as Harold as much as possible, preferring to sit in one of the two Parker Knoll wing armchairs that had now been placed in front of the French windows in the extended dining room, watching the rain trickle down the window panes. Harold usually occupied one of the over-stuffed chairs in the lounge, though inevitably we coincided sometimes. On Sunday mornings, he would sit reading the Sunday Express, wetting his thumb before he used it to turn the pages, in a movement that filled me with revulsion. I would shut my eyes and try to drive away the memory of that sticky thumb moving towards my middle.

In the summer of 1964 we returned to Mallorca, to the same hotel in Cala Mayor, but this time with Rosemary and Hilary in tow, so I did not have to share a room with Harold. He hired a car and we travelled round the island, stopping in Deia, the village that had become famous as the home of the poet Robert Graves, though the villagers told us that Graves was temporarily living in Oxford where he had accepted the post as professor of poetry. Up in the hills at Valldemossa we visited the monastery where the composer Frédéric Chopin and his lover, the novelist George Sand, had stayed. Harold had not the faintest idea who George Sand was and I had to explain that she was in fact a woman, called Amantine-Lucile-Aurore Dupin, who, in common with other female novelists of the period, had felt obliged to use a male pseudonym in order to get published. I sat at Chopin's piano, a rather lovely mahogany-coloured upright infinitely more appealing than the shiny black instrument we had at No. 35, around which Hilary and I, with paper hats from crackers on our heads, were obliged to sing Christmas carols every Christmas, but I refused the suggestion to play a few notes on Chopin's piano. I doubt if it had been kept tuned anyway.

Harold had acquired a very expensive Canon camera prior to this trip and spent a lot of time away from the rest of us using up many rolls of Kodak film snapping local views. He had also purchased a slide projector and screen, which were kept stored in the bogey-hole under the stairs, so when we were back in Eccles he held a series of slide shows for his and Rosemary's friends from the golf club at which I had to feed the transparencies into the projector. After shots of golf courses and the beach at Cala Mayor, followed by views of Deia, Valldemossa and the beautiful coast round Formentor, Harold would pause dramatically and announce, 'And now for the final slide, my masterpiece!' This was my cue to show a very red but otherwise unremarkable sunset which I had been instructed to leave showing for several minutes, 'so the full beauty of it can sink in.' Most of the Fryers' golf club friends were too polite to refuse invitations to these slide shows but the pictures were so banal that I cannot imagine they were genuinely entertained. After the lights were turned back on, I would hand round drinks and plates of bridge rolls filled with shrimps or egg mayonnaise. I was starting to play a convincing act as the dutiful son but all the time I was hating it and plotting how I could get away. After the light supper, the guests would go into the kitchen to do the washing up, which struck me as very inhospitable on the part of Rosemary, but that seemed to be the norm with middle class entertaining; I decided that when I was in the position to have friends of my own round for a meal the dishes would be left to the morning, while we lingered at table with drinks and enjoyed each other's company and conversation deep into the night.

* * *

After I switched to the science side at school, I no longer saw John Jenkins; only many years later did I learn that he had actually left MGS soon after our academic paths separated, having decided it was not for him. But I had made one new friend called Philip, who shared my newly developed passion for cinema. I had taken to going on my own to the Saturday afternoon matinées at the cinema in Monton, where for sixpence you could watch the latest episode of a long-running serial and a few cartoons as well as a full-length feature film. It was there that I saw Disney's animated *101 Dalmatians*, and was so enchanted by it that I sat fixed in my seat when it ended so I could watch it all over again at its second showing. Philip and I were particularly keen to see Don Chaffey's *Jason and the Argonauts* when it came out, having been stirred by a trailer featuring Todd Armstrong battling various challenges as he went in search of the Golden Fleece, so we arranged to go to a huge old cinema in Manchester city centre where it was going to be showing one Saturday afternoon. The cinema was almost empty as we settled into seats on the front row of the balcony, having first bought two vanilla ice-creams. Hardly had the film started before I accidentally dropped my ice-cream over the edge of the balcony; this fell onto the head of a man in the main auditorium below, prompting a howl of outrage. Philip and I looked at each other in horror and fled.

Philip also shared my adolescent fervour for religion, though as an Anglo-Catholic in his case. He was reading up on the Holy Roman Empire and seemed to think that the world had gone downhill ever since then. In the Easter holidays 1965 there was a school trip to Florence and Venice, where there was ample opportunity for both of us to savour the richness of Catholic religious art in galleries such as the Uffizi as well as in numerous churches. Part of Philip's devotion involved quantity as well as quality; on arrival in Venice he announced that there were 39 churches we absolutely had to see. I gave up after about 12 and instead happily stood in St Mark's Square while pigeons covered my head and outstretched arms as I held out corn in my open hands. Despite all the walking in the two cities, I put on even more weight, as I could not resist second helpings of the pasta that was served before the main course at each meal.

Back in Manchester, I wondered if maybe Roman Catholicism was more suitable for me than dourer Anglicanism. There was something intoxicating about the incense and the ritual and the services in Latin (which I still could not understand). So when I saw an advertisement in a newspaper for a free correspondence course in Catholicism from the Catholic Truth Society I sent off for it. Each time a pamphlet arrived I studied it carefully and I started to compose my own prayers and leave them on scraps of paper in my bedroom. Rosemary's nephew Antony, Doreen's son from her second marriage, was studying to be a Catholic priest and I wondered if that might be an option to consider, instead of being a missionary to the Church of South India. Moreover, the concept of confession was greatly appealing; as a Catholic I would be able to confess the sins in which I had been involved in my bedroom and I could be forgiven.

After a few months, the Catholic Truth Society pamphlets stopped arriving. I wondered if Harold had intervened and told them to stop sending them. But as he and I were not really speaking by this stage, I did not feel able to ask.

* * *

In 1965, MGS organised its 450th anniversary celebrations, of which the highlight was a visit to the school by Her Majesty the Queen. She arrived in an enormous maroon Rolls Royce, the upper rear part of which was all made of glass so one could get a good view of the royal personage. All of us boys were lined up along the drive that ran from the front gates to the main quad, shivering in the cold until the Queen's car arrived. As is usual on such occasions, the visit was stage managed to the utmost degree, but the school authorities had not taken the Queen's occasionally impish sense of humour into account. A privileged few of the very brightest and most successful boys had been selected to be introduced to her, as she toured a number of specific classrooms. Along with the rest of S4L, I was shut away in another room for the duration of the visit; we had been instructed to bring a packed lunch from home with us, so the monarch would not be disturbed by the sound or sight of hundreds of boys rushing down to the refectory for lunch. However, just as I had poured myself a cup of Heinz tomato soup from the thermos flask I had brought from No. 35 and was taking a bite out of a barm cake, the door opened and in walked the Queen, saying 'And what do we have in here?', followed by a flustered High Master. Before he could say anything, she caught a whiff of my soup and said, 'That smells good!', before turning on her heels and exiting, happy with her little demonstration of independence.

68

* * *

The only subject at school in which I was not always bottom or next to the bottom in class was music. The music rooms were on the first floor of the cricket pavilion and although most of my friends considered the music lessons to be a waste of time, it was only there that I emerged from the mental torpor in which I spent most of the day, dragging my way round from one class to the next with my fat leather briefcase full of coloured crayons in my hand. The music master played records for us on a gramophone, to illustrate the various musical forms – sonatas, concerti, symphonies and so on. We were given music paper to practise writing melodies and learned the different symbols used as notation in a musical score. Best of all, those of us who expressed more than a casual interest in the subject were allowed to experiment with various musical instruments and if we persuaded the master we really wanted to learn to play one, we could take it home to practise. Given my summer asthma, it seemed wise to avoid a wind instrument in my case and the dreadful screeches produced on violins by novice players set my teeth on edge. So I opted for a cello, which came with its own zip-up khaki canvas case. I was already quite tall for my age and therefore had no great difficulty in moving this bulky instrument around, though struggling onto buses with it in the rush hour was a pain. There was a sort of cubby hole under the stairs on the double-decker buses into which it fitted neatly, though often I had to persuade a disgruntled bus conductor to move out of the way so I could get it in. At least the friendly German conductress on the No. 54 bus back to Eccles approved.

At home, there was the upright piano in the lounge, on which Hilary had learned to play, moving steadily through her grade examinations while at school. A music teacher by the name of Miss Muckley was engaged to teach me to play properly as well; she came to the house once a week. Almost a caricature of a plain, slim spinster in glasses, she struck me as quite a tyrant, insisting on her first visit to the house that Harold must buy an angle-poise lamp to shine on the sheet music, otherwise both she and I would ruin our eyes. To my surprise, meekly he obeyed. The lessons began with the inevitable scales, with Miss Muckley bouncing her pencil on my fingers when I was not holding my hands correctly. Before too long I moved on to the simplest works of Mozart and Clementi, but I quickly got bored with practising the same piece over and over again whenever the room was free, so I started improvising. What I produced was not jazz or anything similarly modern, but rather a pastiche of late German romanticism. I had been taken to hear Sir John Barbirolli conduct the Hallé Orchestra at the Free Trade Hall in Manchester city centre a couple of times and had been profoundly stirred by Mahler, who was then only just starting to come back into fashion, but whose music chimed well with my usual mood of morbid tragedy and gloom. Accordingly, the pieces I was concocting on the piano at home were full of dramatic crescendos and syrupy melodies, some of which I managed to write down in large paper-backed volumes of music sheets.

Miss Muckley tut-tutted when I showed some of the sheets to her and told me I should forget such nonsense and learn to play the piano properly first, something on which I was not making great progress. I don't remember the exact reason for our falling out, either with me directly or with Harold, who was responsible for such decisions, but the lessons with Miss Muckley stopped and instead I was sent to be interviewed for a place as a part-time pupil at the Northern School of Music.

The interview was carried out by the Principal herself, Miss Ida Carroll, a formidable yet fundamentally kindly character approaching 60. We talked about my favourite composers and she sat me down at a grand piano (the first time I had ever touched one). She was pleased I had been learning to play the cello as well, as that was a favourite instrument of hers, along with the double bass. I cannot have played her very much, but whatever it was proved sufficient to persuade her I should be admitted to the School, for a weekly late afternoon lesson in composition, for which I stopped off on my way home from MGS as the Northern School of Music was conveniently located on the bus route from school to central Manchester. My teacher over the coming months was a young Catholic nun who was always dressed in her religious habit. Once she asked me to write a 64-bar waltz for piano. The work I produced (Opus 1.1) was perfect

70

in form but of mind-numbing banality, but the nun was thrilled I had got the first part right, beaming at me from under her wimple.

Although I had my doubts that I would ever be a good pianist, let alone a successful composer, I enjoyed this brief sojourn in the world of music, until one awful afternoon when I was called to the High Master's study at MGS. The High Master, Peter Mason – who had taken over in 1962 from the far more eminent Eric James – was a figure I only knew from seeing him at morning assemblies, tall and slim and seemingly aloof. My fears that I was about to be expelled on account of my dismal academic performance and uncooperative attitude were dispelled by the amused look on the High Master's face as he told me that Harold was on his way to the school to take me to meet someone who might change my life, so I was excused classes for the rest of the day. My mind was racing, trying to imagine what all this was about. When Harold arrived in the car all he said was that we were going to the Free Trade Hall, which struck me as odd, as I did not think the Hallé put on concerts on weekday afternoons. When we had parked the car at the rear of the Midland Hotel, my heart sank when Harold removed from the boot the music sheets that I had been working on at home, which he had taken from the compartment under the seat of the piano stool in the lounge at No. 35. By the time we entered the Free Trade Hall my heart was beating fast and I felt quite faint. We were ushered downstairs to a practice room by a man I vaguely recognised as a neighbour from Chatsworth Road, through whom Harold had obviously arranged this particular surprise. I was told to sit at the upright piano and wait.

Very shortly, in came the Hallé Orchestra's Assistant Conductor, Lawrence Leonard, brisk and business-like in his suit and in his manner. After brief introductions, Harold put my music sheets on the piano and told me to play my latest composition. What he did not know, but I was only too well aware of, was that I had only written about 90 seconds worth of that particular piece. Shakily I played this opening, which had been unashamedly influenced from the first movement of Grieg's piano concerto, and after 90 seconds stopped dead, staring at the next, blank, music sheet. There was an embarrassing silence until Lawrence Leonard very gently suggested that I return in six months' time, having written an original three part invention in the style of Bach. He then shook my hand and left.

Harold was red in the face and as soon as we were out in the street shouted, 'How could you humiliate me like that?'

How could YOU humiliate ME like that?

I never wrote that three part invention. Indeed, I never write another note of music. Harold withdrew me from the Northern School of Music, I stopped borrowing the cello from school, and my interest in the music lessons there evaporated.

* * *

Meanwhile I awaited the results of the 'O' levels I had taken, knowing that they would be dire. At MGS in those days boys were only allowed to take five or maximum six subjects at 'O' level, on the grounds that that was all that was necessary in order to be able to move on to the sixth form and study for 'A' levels. A flimsy added pretext was that the school had to pay a fee to the exam Board for each examination every boy sat, so sitting more 'O' levels than necessary would be a waste of money, or so they said. As I was in S4L, I had to take Physics, Chemistry, Mathematics, English Language and Latin, though I was allowed to add History. My request to sit English Literature was rejected as the school did not think this a serious subject at 'O' level, while my suggestion of Divinity as a subject was met with a hollow laugh. I knew as I sat the papers that I was failing most of them, and I even took a perverse pleasure in ensuring that I got the lowest grade possible in the two sciences. I assumed that when the dreadful results arrived that would be the end of my school days, a prospect I viewed with some excitement. Dire indeed the 'O' levels were and in trying to explain them to Harold and Rosemary, I said (truthfully) that the school had not allowed me to take the subjects I liked and anyway the past five years had been a total waste of time.

That September I put on the last of my charity garden parties, with the help of Hilary, who was home before going to college, and some of her friends. As the Eccles Journal loyally reported, this garden party raised £27 and three shillings (over £490 in 2016 terms), which I channelled to Cancer Research at the Christie Hospital in Manchester. This meant that it was by far the most successful of the events I had put on, but I knew it would be the last. The act of organising these events and the fact that they were always written up in the local paper had acted like a form of self-validation, proving to myself that I was not completely useless, whatever Harold said. I could make things happen, which would be of benefit to others, while at the same time helping me to be a person in my own right. But from now on, I would earn and save money strictly for myself, paying it into my Burnley Building Society account on a regular basis, until I had enough money saved to get away from Eccles and away from school. I had no clear idea where, South India having by now dropped off my radar.

* * *

MGS had meanwhile come up with an alternative to my leaving school with almost no qualifications. Though the vast majority of MGS boys glided gently from 'O'-levels to the sixth form and 'A' levels and from there on to university, there was a special class called 6-Transitus which was designed to cater for boys who had missed long periods at school because of illness or some unfortunate family circumstances, or who, like me, had discovered that their school career so far had been along the wrong path. Accordingly, 6-Transitus was not part of any specific modern, classical or scientific stream and one could more or less choose which subjects one wanted to study. Latin and Maths were still compulsory, but I was now able to tackle French properly, as well as Geography, English Literature and History (again, but with a different syllabus). The history master must have been nearing the end of his working career and had some problem with his prostate, which meant that he had been allocated a teaching room at one end of the History corridor, next door to a toilet, to which he occasionally had to absent himself during class. With the typical subtlety of schoolboys, he was known to all of us as Harry the Bog. I enjoyed the new syllabus which covered the age of European Empires up to the causes of the First World War, but when

I asked Harry why we were not going to study the Great War itself, he replied tartly, 'That isn't history, yet!'

A former army chaplain, a little man with a bald head and lively mind, ran a course on world religions which excited me, as I was now able not just to learn more about far-flung places but what the people there actually believed, what made them and their societies tick. Moreover, despite the stark warning about my perceived lack of ability with languages a few years previously, the fact that I was rapidly improving in French by now encouraged the form master to suggest that I be one of the pupils who should try an experimental Russian course that the school was just starting. Although Nikita Krushchev had been removed from power by his Communist Party colleagues the previous year, some of the relatively liberal reforms that accompanied his de-Stalinisation policies in the late 1950s and early 1960s encouraged several Western countries, including Harold Wilson's Britain, to overcome Cold War fears and develop some degree of engagement. Hence the idea of teaching Russian, of which I soon gained a good basic understanding.

* * *

At home in Eccles, I had started visiting on a regular basis an old woman who lived on her own in the Lodge at the top end of Chatsworth Road. When I had called there the first time in the hope of getting something from her for one of the garden parties I had discovered that she lived in great poverty and squalor, confined to one room that served as both living room and bedroom, heated by a single-bar electric fire. I offered to brighten the place up a bit, later bringing her a tasseled pink lampshade from Fryer's to mask the naked light-bulb that hung from the ceiling and covering her scratched wooden side-table with a sheet of brightly patterned plastic. At Christmas, after eating my own turkey lunch, I packaged up a portion and cycled along the road with it for her. I noticed that she had removed the lampshade I had given her and had ripped off the plastic sheet from the table and she seemed in a grumpy mood. 'That bishop who lives right opposite has never bothered to come to see me once,' she complained. 'Not even at Christmas! So much for

Christian charity!' To my lasting shame, I never plucked up the courage to go to Ted Wickham to suggest he should call on his neighbour and shortly afterwards she must have died or else been moved into a care home, as the Lodge was first boarded up and then knocked down, to be replaced by a small block of flats.

During those Christmas holidays of 1965-1966, I went on a school skiing trip to Kitzbühel in Austria, travelling there by coach through Belgium and Germany. The alpine scenery under deep snow was startlingly beautiful, and to my surprise I discovered that even though I had been useless at sports at MGS and had ensured that I got out of them, I took to skiing immediately. I was able to breathe up on top of the mountains like I had never done before and the sense of exhilaration while skiing downhill was liberating. The exercise obviously did me good as I lost nearly half a stone in weight over the fortnight of the trip. The result was that I returned to Manchester feeling a lot less lethargic and genuinely refreshed. I had also set myself a new challenge. It had been impossible to communicate with the locals in Kitzbühel, who only spoke a heavily accented German, but just as I had been prompted to learn French by the older boy who could converse happily in shops and museums in Paris, so now I realised there was a reason to learn German. Unfortunately, it was not possible to start German from scratch in 6-Transitus, so I found a native German speaker called Frau Spenser who offered private lessons in Eccles and I went to her house twice a week for an hour. As she was interested in music and literature these lessons soon roamed far beyond the curriculum needed for a German O-level, though in principle she was preparing me for that.

* * *

Perhaps it was one of the older boys who had been on the skiing trip to Kitzbühel who encouraged me to go along to hear the Leader of the Liberal Party, Jo Grimond, when he came to address the school as part of a national tour in the run-up to the March 1966 general election. Given that the voting age in Britain was still 21, which meant that even the sixth formers at MGS would not be able to vote for several years, it was something of an altruistic act on Jo

Grimond's part, doubtless arranged through the Old Mancunian GP and TV broadcaster, Dr Michael Winstanley, who was standing as a candidate in the Liberals' target seat of Cheadle. The Liberals had won only nine seats in the 1964 election, when Harold Wilson had led the Labour Party to a narrow victory, and they were able to field candidates in just under half the parliamentary seats in the country in March 1966, but Jo Grimond had a reputation as a fine, radical orator, and he did not disappoint. Indeed, I was metaphorically swept off my feet by what I heard him say, with his championing of civil liberties, internationalism and British membership of the Common Market, as the European Union was called in those days. Everything about him was the complete opposite of the narrow-minded conservatism of Harold Fryer and most of his siblings. Though my revulsion against Harold was primarily physical his political views were an added cause for antagonism. As a businessman, he never made his political affiliation public, but each year the Treasurer of the Eccles Conservative Association would come round to No. 35 to collect a generous cheque. Harold swore at the TV, especially when his namesake Harold Wilson was on, but he did not think much of the new Tory leader, Edward Heath, either. He believed 'RAB' Butler should have been Conservative leader, though in 1968 Harold's allegiance switched firmly to Enoch Powell, after Powell's 'Rivers of Blood' speech in Birmingham about the dangers of immigration, and he started to collect press cuttings about Powell, which he kept in the desk in the dining room. I have no doubt that Harold would have been an eager convert to the United Kingdom Independence Party had he still been alive when UKIP was formed.

I wonder how many other boys in the lecture theatre at MGS in March 1966 were as inspired by Jo Grimond as I was. It was a truly liberating feeling realising that there was a political leader whose views encapsulated what I instinctively believed. Had there been someone with membership forms for the Party I would have signed up on the spot, but when I contacted the Eccles local party shortly afterwards they were distinctly disconcerted about what to do with a 15-year-old enthusiast. I was too young to join the Party, they declared, and currently there was no Young Liberal group in the area. There was not even any use offering help campaigning, as they were not going to fight the parliamentary seat in the General election, and had not done so since 1950, which helped explain why the local association was largely moribund. It was nonetheless galling that the Communist Party was able to field a candidate in the Eccles parliamentary seat in 1966, even if he only polled 1,239 votes, losing his deposit.

There were a couple of Liberal councillors on the borough council in Eccles, but they only got elected because of a pact with the Conservatives, who did not oppose them in their ward, while in return the Liberals did not oppose the Conservatives who had councillors in Ellesmere Park; these included the grocer who delivered Rosemary's order every week in his little van. Otherwise Eccles was a Labour one party state. When I went to meet one of the Liberal councillors to offer help I said I thought Ellesmere Park would be a good place to do some Liberal campaigning, but I was given short shrift. Any such activity would break the pact and then the Conservatives would put up candidates in the Liberal ward which would result in the two Liberal councillors losing their seats, he protested. That is exactly what had happened at the national level in the 1964 general election, when the Liberal MPs for Bolton West and Huddersfield West, against whom the Conservatives had previously not fielded candidates, lost their seats when the Tories entered the field. This rebuff temporarily put a dampener on my new political enthusiasm, though inwardly I celebrated when the Liberals made a net gain of three seats on 31 March, one of the 12 victors being Michael Winstanley in Cheadle. Harold Wilson had increased his majority in the House of Commons to a healthy 98, which left his namesake at No. 35 thunderous.

* * *

Meanwhile my French was coming on particularly well thanks to a twinning arrangement that Eccles had with the town of Narbonne in the south of France. This involved schoolchildren as well as adults and in the Easter break 1966 I went to stay with the family of a boy called Maurice, whose father was the equivalent of town clerk of the town. The Mediterranean weather was already balmy and after the

77

family had picked me up from Perpignan airport we had a late lunch at their airy modern apartment. The first course was half a cantaloupe melon, whose centre had been relieved of its seeds and filled with port. This was my first experience of alcohol and I was pleasantly surprised, though I thought I had probably better not tell Harold and Rosemary I had tried it. In those days, youths under the age of 18 were not even allowed into British pubs.

Maurice and I did not particularly get on; his idea of fun was to try to set fire to ants' nests by dropping lighted paper down the entrance hole. But I liked his father and was enchanted by his grandfather who lived in a village quite far away from Narbonne. One weekend we all went to stay in the grandfather's house where he showed me all the sheets of stamps he had saved from when he worked for the local post office; though I asked him not to, he tore corners off these sheets for me to take home to add to my collection. He kept rabbits in a hutch in the garden, but I was dismayed when one of them appeared on the dining room table as our dinner. However, my strongest memory of that visit is of a lunch in the village to celebrate some infant's baptism. Tables and chairs were arranged outside, and large jugs of wine were liberally spread around. The meal lasted all afternoon, as course after course was brought out by the womenfolk. I was struck by the fact that the meat was served on its own, with a sauce, while the vegetables came separately later. All the time, the people round the tables were telling stories and laughing at jokes, as small children and dogs ran around, the whole scene bathed in a golden southern light. It was all a million miles away from life in Eccles, so vibrant and jolly. When Maurice's parents told us it was time to drive back to Narbonne, I was sad and would happily have been left behind.

* * *

In July 1966, the population of England was seized with World Cup fever, including Harold at No. 35. He was a longstanding fan of Manchester United and had never really recovered from the shock of the February 1958 Munich air crash, in which eight players on the team had been killed. Nonetheless, he liked to watch United's

78

matches on TV and was inordinately proud of the fact that the BBC's football commentator, Kenneth Wolstenholme, who hailed from Worsley, had lived in Chatsworth Road before moving down south. Wolstenholme's voice dominated the household in the second half of July and Harold was excited that three of the World Cup matches were going to be played at Old Trafford, Manchester United's ground. Although he knew I had absolutely no interest in football he insisted in taking me to see the Bulgaria versus Hungary match on 20 July, saying 'it will be good for you.'

We had seats but were located so far back in the stand that I could not see the ball and I soon got bored just watching the players running around. I was also starting to feel cold. As both teams came from Communist countries there was no great groundswell of support for either side among the crowd and I could not have cared less about which side might win. Harold was rooting for Hungary on the grounds that the Hungarians had risen up against their Soviet oppressors 10 years before, so he was pleased they won 3:1. But there was no way of hiding my sullen indifference. 'Do you realise how much these seats cost?' he snapped, as we pushed our way back through the crowds to the car. I had longed since stopped responding to such questions and we drove home in silence. Rather than listen to him complaining about me to Rosemary when we reached No. 35, I went straight up to my room.

His anger with me faded as over the next 10 days he got caught up in the national excitement as the English team progressed steadily towards the final, which was held at Wembley on 30 July. Both Harold and Rosemary were among the 32 million Britons who sat in front of the television to watch the match. I stayed in the garden but I could hear the commentary coming through the open windows of our neighbours' houses as well as our own. The roar every time England scored was tremendous but I found myself shutting my ears to what was going on, feeling out of place not just at No. 35 and Eccles but in the country as a whole. So I missed Kenneth Wolstenholme's legendary comment, 'they think it's all over ... well it is now!' Rosemary came rushing out of the French windows, shouting, 'We won! We won! We beat Germany, 4:2!' I closed my eyes and mentally disappeared.

* * *

One of the first things Harold Wilson did that summer was to introduce tight exchange controls, which meant that British travellers were only allowed to take £50 out of the country in spending money each year outside the sterling area. The Prime Minister himself patriotically favoured the Scilly Islands for his holidays, thus obviating his need for foreign cash. The amounts of foreign currency one collected from banks or exchange bureaux were entered onto a page at the back of one's passport. Having decided that I was going to spend as much time in continental Europe as possible I was not at all happy at the prospect at having my wings clipped by government restrictions, always assuming I could raise the money to do the sort of travel I was dreaming of. Accordingly, I wrote a letter about the matter to the Manchester Evening News, without letting on that I was a 16-year-old schoolboy: 'Although Mr Wilson has come out with his latest method to stop spending abroad with the cut in currency allowances for holidays, he has forgotten to tell us where exactly we can go on holiday without such restrictions (other than the Scilly Islands, that is). Perhaps you can enlighten us?' Below my letter the Editor posted a helpful response: 'The cut applies to travel outside the sterling area. A travel agency official says: "The restriction does not apply – as well as the United Kingdom, of course – to the Channel Islands, Eire, Gibraltar, Iceland, the Isle of Man, Malta and many countries further afield such as Ceylon, Burma, Hong Kong, India, Jordan, Kuwait, Pakistan and the Bahamas."' That final sentence sent my mind into overdrive, as I reached for the Encyclopaedia Britannica Atlas and started to plan imaginary travels to the Middle East and Asia.

For once Harold and I were on the same wavelength as he was equally determined not to have his wings clipped by Mr Wilson. As an act of defiance, and to mark his 65th birthday, he arranged for Rosemary, Hilary and I to go over to France with him for a month in August – the last such family holiday together – with clandestine stashes of five pound notes secreted in various items of luggage. The trip was arranged at quite short notice, once Rosemary had declared that she wanted to visit the Riviera again, to see if it had changed since she was a girl. The journey involved driving down to one of the South Coast ferries in the Daimler then once in France putting the car on an overnight sleeper train to Lyon. In Lyon we checked into a rather grand old hotel, where Rosemary complained of the heat and immediately fell ill with some infection. A doctor was summoned who spoke no English, so I acted as interpreter and was later despatched to the nearest chemist's to collect the prescribed medicine, which was contained in glass ampoules that I was given charge of cutting open with a razor blade. Harold, who hated not to be in control, had seemingly evaporated. This nonetheless left me with a lot of free time to order what I wanted in the restaurant – usually coquille St.-Jacques – and to wander round the city, with its glorious 15th century cathedral.

We were stuck in Lyon for several days until Rosemary was well enough to travel, which meant that our itinerary had to change and we would not be going to the Riviera after all, as we had a booking on a ferry from Cherbourg back to England on a specific date. This was a disappointment to both Hilary and me; I had imagined running into Brigitte Bardot in St.-Tropez. But we did manage to see beautiful cities such as Avignon and Albi before heading north to Poitiers and the Loire Valley. Harold suddenly decided that he wanted to use up his remaining stash of sterling to buy some antiques to take home, which took me by surprise as until then the only real antiques in the house had been the inherited small Russian trove. In Poitiers, he accordingly acquired a rather fine metal sculpture of a group of troubadours performing in the street and a rococo green porcelain vase adorned with white cherubs. These were then wrapped in rugs and hidden under Hilary's and my feet in the hope that the British customs would not find them, which fortunately they did not.

Because Harold had passed official retirement age he started winding down his work at Fryer's and some of the younger generation of the family were now being given greater responsibilities, though that did not stop Harold grumbling about them when he came home from increasingly infrequent visits to the store. It had never been suggested that I join the firm, which is probably as well; as a recently politicised teenager I took a dim view of 'business'. From Harold's point of view, once he was no longer one of the men in charge Fryer's went downhill. Indeed, its fortunes did decline over the next few years, but that was largely because of a change in people's shopping habits away from high street department stores to out-of-town shopping centres. What finally killed the business off, however, was the construction of a motorway that sliced right through the centre of Eccles, turning the top end of Church Street into a cul-de-sac and cutting the shop off from its more affluent customers in Ellesmere Park. One irony of this situation, which would lead to the company going into ignominious bankruptcy and the main Eccles store itself being turned into a Woolworth's, was that Harold had a passion for motorways, mainly because he could let rip on them in his Daimler. Motorways also appealed to his peculiar sense of aesthetics and his national pride. Germany had long had its autobahn network and Harold was excited when the M6 motorway was at last being built to the west of Eccles, driving Rosemary and I off there one afternoon to have a look at it under construction. While I stared down at the machines laying tarmac, thinking what an ugly scar was being sliced through the landscape, he was rhapsodising about it as the new 'Backbone of Britain'.

* * *

When the exam results came through the post they showed that the year in 6-Transitus had done its job effectively. I had passed without difficulty my 'O'-levels in English Language, French, Geography, History and Maths and even managed to scrape through Latin, largely by learning translated passages of the set book, Julius Caesar's *The Conquest of Gaul*, off by heart. Fortunately MGS saw the funny side of how things had developed academically and were happy to welcome me into the sixth form in September 1966, with the agreement that I would study for English Literature, French and Geography at 'A'-level and English and Geography at 'S'-level – the latter being seen as a stepping stone towards the examinations to enter Oxford or Cambridge.

In contrast to the masters who had failed to arouse me from my mental distraction in my earlier years at Manchester Grammar, the sixth form teachers were for the most part real stars, who made their subjects exciting and ensured that the pupils were engaged. I remember particularly one of the French masters, David Nott (who would later proceed me as a Non-Executive Director of the Authors Licensing and Collecting Society, ALCS) who initiated me, through *La Symphonie pastorale*, into a passion for André Gide. When I came across Gide's famous quote, 'Familles, je vous hais!'(Families, I hate you!), I shouted out loud, 'Yes!' Yet even more stimulating was the work of Albert Camus, whose *L'Etranger* was one of the set books for 'A'-level. I empathised with the narrator Mersault's failure to cry at his mother's funeral (given how distant I felt from my adoptive mother, Rosemary) as well as his inability to feel emotions about the people around him. Common to both Gide and Camus, of course, was the dramatic sense of place, in particular French Algeria – this was the appeal of the exotic but their books also conveyed an enticing atmosphere of strange cruelty in Arab lands.

Oddly I felt more detached from the English literature classes, possibly because Shakespeare formed such an important part of the curriculum, notably *Othello* and *Antony and Cleopatra*, and I felt I had grown out of Shakespeare (ah, the arrogance of youth!). In previous years I had revelled in school Shakespeare productions, notably the King Lear in which Robert Powell played the title role, and I had even won a £2 Shakespeare Scholarship prize, the only prize I ever won at MGS. But my tastes had moved on to more modern texts in both drama and novels, in particular relishing the plays of Arnold Wesker and Eugene Ionesco, which a group of us from school went to see at the Green Room Theatre in Manchester. I would feel a heightened sense of emotion while watching an excellent production of a play and became convinced that my destiny was to become a writer, to move other people by the power of words. Although I had continued writing bits and pieces for my own pleasure ever since the little story about the cat I now determined to compose something for publication and wrote a more solid piece of short fiction, originally conceived as a novella but which ended up as a short story, rather pretentiously called *A Wheel of Many Colours*, which was published in the school magazine, Ulula.

One boy in our English class declared a passion for the novels of Virginia Woolf, who was only starting to come back into fashion, prompting howls of derision from the English master. That master, Brian Phythian, had clear favourites among the pupils, boys he felt were destined for great things, but I was not one of them. The boy who sat next to me for a year, Howard Davies (future Director of the London School of Economics and Chairman of the Royal Bank of Scotland, among many other prestigious positions) certainly was a favourite, and under Mr Phythian's protective guidance he became the founder-editor of the MGS school newspaper, The Mancunian. It was therefore he who commissioned the very first non-fiction article of mine that appeared in print, on 8 December 1966, headlined 'Psychologist talks on E.S.P.' This reported on a meeting of the school's Chi Rho Group (a religious studies society that I was involved with) that had been addressed by a Mr Christiansen, assistant lecturer in psychology at Manchester University, on the subject of extra-sensory perception. 'The talk was well regulated,' the budding journalist in me observed, 'intelligible and interesting, though not inspired. In fact, he opened up a wider field than the title might suggest, and when on the subject of hallucinations and other figments of the imagination, he was on surer and happier ground.' However, there was a sting in the tail of my article: 'Most people left satisfied, although some did leave half was through the meeting.'

Perhaps if I had had more encouragement from Mr Phythian I would have tried to infiltrate the little groups that he had round to his house out of school hours, but as he did not seem interested in me, perhaps because of my chequered school career that far, I did not make the effort. Besides, I had become captivated by the geography lessons, not so much by morphology and climatology but by the economic and human geography of France, which we studied in great depth. This fitted in well with my French language studies so I was soon consulting French language sources for my geography homework and devouring the Petit Larousse concise encyclopaedia. I had also acquired a dark green stamp album just for stamps from

France, which had little spaces marked out for each stamp as well as black-and-white illustrations of many of them.

* * *

On 1 January, 1967, I started writing a diary, as I would continue to do, on and off, for the next 40 years or so. The first volume was a page-a-day affair, bound in blue leather and each day was rated with between one and five stars, ranging from "bad day" to "exceptional". During winter weekends, when I was often confined to the house, as the rain lashed against the glass panes of the French windows, there were a lot of one star days, on which I noted that I was too depressed to do anything other than watch television. Few dates were awarded more than two stars, as I still felt I was time-serving in Eccles. However, the year began well as I was in Austria once again on a skiing trip with other boys from MGS, housed in the same large wooden chalet hotel in Kitzbühel as the year before. Even better than the skiing, which had lost some of its novelty, were the side trips by coach that were laid on, including a day in Salzburg, where I explored the castle and wandered round the cathedral on my own, before we all headed up to Berchtesgaden, where Adolf Hitler had his Eagle's Nest. Standing outside looking in, I could imagine the Führer gazing out over the landscape below him, Master of all he surveyed.

A week later, the coach took us to Munich, where we boarded an overnight train that was crowded with Yugoslav migrant workers heading north. A missed boat connection at Ostend meant that I wasn't back in Manchester for another 24 hours, whiling away the time by reading *Eugénie Grandet*, Honoré de Balzac's novel about miserliness, in which the father inevitably reminded me of Harold. Though he earned a reasonable salary from Fryer's and had large shareholdings, Harold grumbled about every penny he had to spend and swore that the Labour government was trying to bleed him dry through high taxes. When I got back to Eccles, he was in bed, coughing and spluttering with his emphysema, demanding to have Vicks rubbed into his chest and back. I had to shut my eyes while I was doing that, moving my sticky hands over his flabby carcass, while he barked, 'Harder! Harder!' Had it not been for the astringent smell of the medication I would probably have passed out.

Not for the first time, thinking of others worse off than myself helped me avoid slipping quickly back into deep depression. On 11 January, taking advantage of the fact that Harold was still laid up in bed, I watched Jeremy Sanford and Ken Loach's *Cathy Come Home* on the TV. In the television play, a young couple and their small child are evicted from their comfy home by bailiffs after the husband is injured and loses his job and from then on there is a descending spiral of unemployment, squatting and homelessness. One commentator later called the programme 'an ice pick in the brain of all that saw it', and certainly it shook me. I began to wonder that if I did run away from No. 35 and couldn't earn a living, maybe I would end up on the streets as well.

Is that what had happened to my mother? Where might she have ended up now? Does she have a husband or is she all alone? Is she homeless?

I had better keep my head down and make sure I can stand on my own feet when eventually I do cut and run.

* * *

Some months later, a very blond 17-year-old German youth called Ulrich Schultz came over from Essen to stay at No. 35 through another town twinning programme. He was extremely polite, but he sensed the odd atmosphere at the house, where Harold and Rosemary barely addressed a word to him, or indeed to each other. I suppose that must have been partly because the lad was German but there was more to it than that. Rosemary's behaviour was beginning to get ever more eccentric and Harold was becoming more nervous about her condition. 'You do not like your father,' Ulrich declared with Teutonic directness towards the end of his stay in Eccles. 'No,' I replied. But I was not prepared to go into the reasons why with someone I barely knew.

When I went over to stay with Ulrich's parents the following Easter in their neat little apartment in Essen the atmosphere was completely different. I was conscious that 90 per cent of the centre of the city had been destroyed by Allied bombing during the War; most families, like Ulrich's, lived in functional modern blocks, though Essen's economy was booming thanks to industrial regeneration, in stark contrast to Manchester, which was sinking into post-industrial gloom. Harold has instructed me to ask Ulrich's father what he had done during the War, but I did not, as the whole point of the twinning exercise was to foster reconciliation and mutual understanding, not to reopen old wounds. The stay with Ulrich certainly helped my German come along, but it was my Eccles German language teacher, Frau Spenser, with her stories of Goethe and Schiller, who ensured I got through my German 'O'-level (entrance fee paid for by myself) not long afterwards.

* * *

In early 1967, Harold and Rosemary went abroad on their own for a while as he was finding it increasingly difficult to cope with winter weather. The suitcases of silver were taken to the Bank and the house was locked up and I was farmed out to stay with Auntie Ruth. Ruth's invalid aunt had died but Ruth still had one of the dachshunds. She was also still working in the health service but cooked me breakfast every morning before I went to school. This was a noble act, seeing that she had never had a husband or children, though of course she had looked after 'Auntie' for years. I was now sleeping in Auntie's bed, which had pink nylon sheets that felt strange against my skin and sometimes crackled with static electricity when I climbed into bed.

Ruth had a friend in the neighbourhood who bred pedigree golden retrievers and I instantly fell in love with the breed when I went over to see them. When Harold and Rosemary returned to England, I mithered Rosemary for weeks to let me have one from the next litter of puppies. Rationally this was an absurd proposition, as the dog would have to be kennelled when they went away in the winter again, which they had decided they would probably do. I think Rosemary felt obliged to agree because of what had happened to my last pet animals. These had been a pair of white mice which I had bought along with a red metal cage, which had a closed compartment for them to sleep in and a much larger barred area for them to eat and play. I put this cage in my room over the garage, but Rosemary soon complained that the mice smelled, insisting that I move them onto the flat roof of the car port. It was easy to climb out of the front window of my bedroom to change the mice's food and water; in fact, I soon discovered that by standing on a chair I could just lean out of the window and do what was necessary without climbing outside. If the mice were in their sleeping compartment at the time they invariably came rushing out when they heard me open the widow. But one morning, after a sharp frost, they did not appear. I climbed out onto the car port roof and gingerly opened the lid of the sleeping area. There in the middle of a bed of straw were the corpses of the mice, frozen to death in a solid white block as they had clung together, their teeth bared. Rosemary undoubtedly felt guilty about this, but maybe the thing that clinched the matter of the dog was when I announced that either we would have a golden retriever puppy or I would leave. As far as I was concerned, that was a win-win situation, and I rather hoped that I would indeed soon be leaving.

Once Auntie Ruth's friend had another litter available I went round to choose one of the puppies. It was a female, all soft and cuddly and sweet-smelling and I called her Tonya, after the wife of Dr Zhivago in the novel by Boris Pasternak. I had not yet read that novel, but like many people I had been swept away by the romance of David Lean's 1965 film version, starring Omar Sharif (as the doctor), Julie Christie (as his love interest, Lara) and Geraldine Chaplin as the doctor's wife, Tonya. I saw the film several times and repeatedly played the theme tune on the stereo that Harold had bought himself for his 65th birthday. Though we did not study Russian literature at MGS, the Russian language teacher told us that the greatest novels ever were written in that language.

Tonya the dog would prove to be a problem, not just because she did indeed have to be sent to kennels when Harold and Rosemary were away, but also because every male dog in the district laid siege to No. 35 each time she went on heat. When that happened, she would make a weird noise and drag her hind quarters along the kitchen floor, leaving a little trail of blood on the yellow linoleum squares behind her. Worse still, she howled to be let out each morning as soon as Rosemary went downstairs to make a cup of tea. Rosemary duly let her out, after which Tonya would wee on the lawn – which was increasingly covered in unsightly brown patches as a result – and then position herself at the front gate where she would bark for minutes on end. The neighbours complained repeatedly about being woken up by this barking, which I was annoyed about too. Eventually, Rosemary contacted Auntie Ruth's friend and had Tonya taken away. Now it was my turn to feel guilty.

* * *

1967 was an exciting year for anyone who was liberal-minded, as the Labour Home Secretary, Roy Jenkins, oversaw the introduction of a number of progressive reforms across a wide range of social policy. One of the hot topics in the newspapers and on radio and TV during the first half of the year was the Sexual Offences Bill that Jenkins was trying to steer through the House of Commons. There had been previous attempts to decriminalise homosexuality between consulting adults, notably by the Welsh Labour MP Leo Abse and the Conservative peer, the 8th Earl of Arran, known as 'Boofy' to his friends. Lord Arran and his wife were both campaigners for animal rights, and he once remarked memorably that he had just two interests in life: 'to stop people buggering badgers and to stop badgering buggers.' There was still a great deal of hostility to the possibility of a Buggers' Charter, as some apoplectic Tory MPs from the shires referred to the measure, claiming that it was designed to protect 'pimps, pansies and queers', but thanks to government support and the tenacity of the bill's proposers, the measure did eventually pass and the subsequent Act legalising homosexual acts in private between two males over the age of 21 was given the Royal Assent towards the end of July. When Lord Arran was asked why he thought this measure had succeeded whereas another bill on protecting badgers that he had backed had failed, he quipped, 'Not many badgers in the House of Lords!'

I remember vividly a television news item about the issue as the bill was being debated, when Rosemary declared vehemently as she stared the screen, 'If I was married to one of them, I would divorce him!' From where I was sitting Harold was also in my sightline and he visibly blanched. Despite all that had happened when I was a child it had never occurred to me that he might be attracted to other men, though it had struck me as odd that he went misty-eyed whenever Cliff Richard came on the TV.

By coincidence, the matter of homosexual desire was something I had been thinking about a lot over the previous weeks. On 4 June, the eve of my 17th birthday, I had gone to visit one of the officers of a constituency Liberal Party association in a different part of Manchester to offer help, as the Eccles association was such a washout. The man was welcoming, sat me down on a sofa next to him and told me that they had a few active Young Liberals in their association who I could work with, as well as helping the association to campaign in preparation for the next local elections. He then suddenly pulled a male physique magazine out from under the cushion he was sitting on and passed them to me, asking if I liked it, as he patted my knee. I demurred and moved away at which point he became very flustered. I said I must be getting home as I wanted to be on good form as I was going to celebrate my 17th birthday the following day by taking my first driving lesson. It suddenly dawned on him how much younger I was than I looked, and that he had taken a very foolish risk, but I assured him I really did not mind and anyway nothing of any significance had happened. He then told me that one of the other members of the local association had recently been let out of prison having served a sentence for gross indecency, the offence for which Oscar Wilde had been jailed for two years in 1895 not all that long after the crime was added to the statute books. I was astonished to learn that people were still being sent to prison as a result of their sexual orientation, which seemed manifestly unjust, so long as both parties consented. I was pleased that Jo Grimond – who had resigned the party leadership in January, being replaced by Jeremy Thorpe – and most of the Liberals backed the overdue reform.

* * *

To improve my French I enrolled for a short summer course at the Institut tourain of the University of Poitiers in Tours. The town was reputed to have the best pronunciation in France and was located in one of the most beautiful and historically interesting parts of the country, which had greatly appealed when we had passed through the previous summer. There were a number of spectacular chateaux along the banks of the Loire that could be visited easily on day trips when French drivers were willing to stop for young hitch-hikers, which wasn't always the case. The teaching methods at the institute were very different from the lessons at MGS. Great emphasis was put on dictation, when the severe French teacher would slowly read out a passage of prose which one had to write down as correctly as possible, including all the accents. This was actually harder than one might imagine. On the other hand, in the examination that came at the end of the course one was allowed to take in one's Petit Larousse to consult while answering essay questions, which struck me as being eminently sensible.

I lodged in the house of a matronly French widow, whose establishment was far more modest than her elegant demeanor. Only two other paying guests were in residence: another English lad of whom I saw little and an older, gangly young American call Jeff, who was immersing himself in the works of Marcel Proust. I was too young to be a companion for him on his evenings out in the cafés and bars of Tours, but we did meet up in his room from time to time to laugh at our landlady's eccentricities. She had stuck up little handwritten notices all over the house, reminding us to turn off the light or lock the front door, or to make sure that the taps in the washbasin were screwed tightly shut. But I think she must have had quite an impish sense of humour, or else one of her previous lodgers did, because there was a tiny notice affixed to the cistern of the lavatory, high up on the wall, which I was only able to read by climbing up on the toilet seat. I was then able to make out the words (in French), 'It is forbidden to climb on the toilet seat.'

* * *

The atmosphere was poisonous when I got back to Eccles; Harold and I had an argument, probably about politics, almost the moment I walked through the door of No. 35, after we had dinner at the Airport Hotel at Manchester Ringway with Rosemary, Hilary – who had just finished college – and the Fryers' favourite bridge and golfing partners, Julia and Den. So I spent much of the remains of that summer far away from the house, birdwatching around Worsley. Deep in the woods there was a beautiful half-timbered hunting and fishing lodge called The Aviary that the first Earl of Ellesmere had had built and which I stumbled upon by accident. To me it was as enchanted a place as any in a fairy story by the Brothers Grimm. I asked the owner, John Prestwich, who I ran into while I was walking, for permission to go birding in the grounds, to which he readily assented, but soon I became much more fascinated by the humans living in The Aviary than in the birds outside. It was a substantial property, built round a courtyard, with outbuildings that served as storage for 'props' which John Prestwich hired out to television companies, as well as housing a handsome young male lodger. John Prestwich was usually out and about when I called, which I did with increasing frequency, especially when I was able to borrow Rosemary's Mini (in which I had successfully passed my driving test at the first attempt) for the afternoon, whereas his wife Pat was almost always at home.

The main room with its large open fireplace smelt strongly of the numerous pugs that ran around the place on their knobbly little legs, snuffling through their squashed noses. The furniture was old but eclectically bohemian and the whole house was as lived in and shabby but comfortable as a pair of favourite shoes. What excited me most, however, was that this was a house with books, not just books that the Prestwiches were reading but a proper working library, with various volumes open at pages that were being consulted as well as notebooks and scraps of paper covered with notes. As she explained, for years Pat had been working on a cache of letters sent between Marcel Proust, his intimate friend, the composer and musician Reynaldo Hahn, and Hahn's British cousin Marie Nordlinger, from whom Pat Prestwich had inherited the correspondence. Many years later, this would form the basis of Pat's book *The Translation of*

92

Memories: Recollections of the Young Proust. It was liberating to be with someone who could talk knowledgably about books, and who empathised so closely with fin de siècle Paris. Taking about Proust – of whom I had still not read a word – fuelled the passion I felt for France and all things French; I even wished I could be French, creating a new identity for myself. As I had been given names that were not originally my own, why should I not in turn give myself some as well? I thought 'Casimir' had a particularly fine ring to it, and started practising it as a signature.

John and Pat were the most exciting people I had ever met and I visited the house and grounds probably more often than I should have, though Pat was never less than welcoming. In contrast to the atmosphere at No. 35, where everything was presented as black or white, right or wrong, respectable or disgusting, at The Aviary everything was a legitimate topic for discussion and sexual orientation was viewed as an inherent element of personality, without any form of condemnatory judgment. I was intrigued by the way the Prestwiches had crafted almost separate lives within their marriage, each pursuing their own interests and different tastes, and I envied their daughter growing up in such a liberal household. It seemed unfair that I hadn't been adopted by a couple like the Prestwiches, as my whole childhood would have been so different. But of course that would never have happened as they had a child of their own.

* * *

The other welcoming place I visited regularly that summer and over the next few years was Stafford House, an imposing Victorian dwelling in Ellesmere Park, which has now been turned into a residential care home, but which in the 1960s was the residence of Mr and Mrs Isherwood of Isherwood's garages. Mr Isherwood could not have been very much older than Harold, yet in my eyes he and his wife became surrogate grandparents, always ready to provide tea and cake and gentle chatter in their elegant and comfortable main sitting room, he having long since retired. Sometimes I would lie in bed at No. 35 and dream that the Isherwoods would adopt me. If one could be adopted once why not twice, especially if the first experience had been unsatisfactory? Indeed, why can adults adopt children but not the other way round? Why couldn't a miserable and lonely child build his own family from the adults available nearby? That is indeed how I would proceed over the following decades, forming emotional ties with older men and women that were far stronger than anything I ever felt for Harold and Rosemary. I told the Isherwoods once that I would have loved to be a part of their family, without mentioning how unhappy I was with the Fryers, and they smiled, clearly pleased.

* * *

When I returned to MGS in September 1967, as a member of the sixth form, the experience of school was transformed. A purpose-built Sixth Form Block (subsequently turned into a language centre) had been constructed on the front side of the main building and this had an atmosphere completely different from the institutional feel of the rest of the school. There was a common room for the use of the sixth-formers, with comfy modern easy chairs and coffee making facilities, as well as small rooms that could be used for seminars. The idea, probably based on practices at public schools, was to make us feel that we were in transition from school to university, not least those one year above me, who were preparing to sit their Oxford or Cambridge entrance exams the following March. They were even allowed to wear ordinary clothes, rather than school uniform.

The way the classes were run in the Sixth Form was different, too, being far more inter-active. For six years I and my diverse classmates had been talked at by teachers, and we all knew that the way to do well in exams was to reproduce what one had been told. But now education had become more of a two-way street, beginning a familiarisation with argument and counter-argument that would be a feature of university-level study. Several of the Masters were notably younger than their colleagues in charge of lower forms, which made two-way communication easier. I became particularly close to one of the two geography masters as he also had a strong interest in politics, which he was happy to talk about outside class. In fact, he sat on a Conservative Party policy working group, which sometimes meant he had to go down to London for meetings. One day he returned from one of those meetings where he had encountered the ambitious MP for Finchley, Margaret Thatcher, fresh from an International Visitor Leadership Program in the United States. This encounter prompted him to declare passionately to me, 'That woman has got to be stopped!' Unfortunately, it would take another 20-odd years for that to happen.

The fact that my sixth form masters were in the main inspiring undoubtedly helped change my attitude to study, but so did the subject matter. It was fortunate that a key element of the geography syllabus was the human geography of France, which I by now viewed as my spiritual home. The French hexagon became imprinted in my mind and gradually I could not only draw from memory a detailed map showing all the main cities, rivers and physical features but also rattle off the major economic activities of each of the country's regions, including the overseas departments.

Back at No. 35, I then altered the way I organised my evenings to get as much studying done while avoiding Harold and Rosemary as much as possible. I no longer loitered in the centre of Manchester on my way back to Eccles but instead went straight to bed when I got to No. 35 and slept until called down for tea. After the meal, which never lasted more than 30 minutes, Harold and Rosemary retired to the lounge to watch television – the Black and White Minstrel Show was Harold's particular favourite – while I covered the dining table with my books. In France, I had bought a French college atlas that had dozens of maps of the country illustrating every imaginable feature, from climate to industry and I never tired of pouring over it for hours. I played records by Charles Aznavour and Edith Piaf on the stereo to drown out the sound of the TV in the next room, wrote French essays that were usually far longer than the required number of words and grunted when Rosemary put her head round the door to say goodnight. I rarely went up to bed before 1am. I had an alarm clock now, set for 7.30am, which meant I just had time to brush my teeth and grab a piece of toast before going now eagerly to school, before Harold had even stirred from his room.

By this stage, about the only time I saw Harold was at mealtimes but I had mastered the technique of pretending he was not there. I still had to sit opposite him, but I no longer had to look over his head to avoid being put off my food. I was now able to look straight through him, as if he was a ghost, though a ghost who had not yet been laid to rest. Unlike Rosemary, usually he did not put his head round the door that linked the lounge to the dining room where I did my evening studies, to say goodnight, but instead went straight out through to the hall and up the stairs to his bedroom when he felt tired. However, one evening when I was busy writing an essay, after Rosemary had already retired, he did come in to the dining room. When I looked up, surprised, he asked me, 'Are you ever physically attracted to men?'

No, no, no. No way am I going to let you off the hook, to allow you to think that somehow what you did was alright. And as you stand there, those fat pink fingers hanging down by your side I can sense inside my head that spider coming towards me, slowly but persistently, and there is no way that I can stop it.

'No,' I lied.

He shrugged and went off to bed. I could no longer concentrate on my homework but sat there just shaking for an hour until I was able to clear my thoughts.

Getting away from here is the only way I will save my sanity.

* * *

At least school was no longer part of the problem. I was actually enjoying it for once and I had even found a friend, a kind of kindred spirit, who was interested in many of the things I was interested in – other than the politics – and was also something of a loner. Much shorter than me and very blond, Roger had very prominent lips, which made him a natural for playing the flute. Moreover, while I had abandoned music-making he had persevered and we enjoyed sometimes going to Hallé concerts together. Although he lived the other side of the Manchester Ship Canal I sometimes used to go round to visit him, partly to get away from No. 35 but mainly because we could talk about literature and films.

One Monday morning at school, while we were all waiting for the English Literature master to arrive, one of my classmates – a

96

handsome lad who was good at sports – astonished us all by informing us he had had sex with his girlfriend the previous Saturday night. There was no reason to disbelieve him yet it did seem an amazing thing to me that any girl who was not 'on the game' would have sex with a boy before marriage, unless she was Swedish. The Swinging Sixties had certainly not yet reached Ellesmere Park. As for myself, on a few occasions I had invited out a rather pretty girl I had met through the Liberal Party and one sunny afternoon I had borrowed Rosemary's Mini Priscilla and driven the girl up onto the moors on the Pennines where we rolled around a bit in the grass and kissed, but that was as far as it went and was as far as either of us would have wanted it to go. But what my classmate told me left me troubled and I kept thinking about it that night as I lay in bed and no amount of praying to God would drive those thoughts away, and because they would not go away I started to question the existence of God. Had I not begged him for forgiveness for my lewd thoughts and asked him to smooth the passage to a pure life in service to humanity? And what had been His response? Zilch.

I bought a paperback copy of D. H. Lawrence's *Lady Chatterley's Lover*, in the hope that this might bring some form of carnal enlightenment, but I found it heavy going; it took me six months to finish the book, writing dejectedly in my diary on its completion, 'Very strange book – quite good (and entertaining!!) in parts, but rather boring & nauseating in others.' By now at least I did understand that one's John Thomas had to be inserted into a woman's cunt (a new word that Lawrence had helpfully added to my vocabulary) for heterosexual congress to take place, but that prospect did indeed strike me as nauseating. Yet I knew I had to do something about the hunger that was starting to gnaw away at my innards, even though there was no girl I could reasonably ask and there was no way I was going to approach one of the working women who by now I knew hung about the streets near the canal in central Manchester at night. Accordingly, I decided to approach a short, lithe gay man in his 30s whom I had also met through the Liberals – though not the one who had tried to seduce me a few months before – and went to see him to ask him if we could give it a go. We went upstairs to his bedroom where I took off my clothes and lay flat on my back on the bed, motionless and unaroused, waiting for him to fiddle with me, as I thought that is what sex between two men was. Unsurprisingly, he quickly got bored and got up, saying rather crossly, 'I don't think you are really into this.' I said sorry, got dressed and left. In fact I was relieved that nothing had really happened. Half a century later, I still can't bear anyone touching me down there.

* * *

Every third weekend throughout most of 1967 and 1968, Rosemary and I drove over to Chesterfield to stay with her mother, Ethel Bishop, née Eyre, grand-daughter of the founder of the well-established Chesterfield firm of furnishers, Eyres, and therefore a cousin to William Fryer's wife Martha. Ethel was known by the Fryers at No. 35 as Brown Grandma, not only to distinguish her from Black Grandma, Martha, but also because she did indeed wear brown clothes most of the time, as well as favouring chiffon and silk scarves patterned with tiny autumn flowers and leaves. In her prime she had been a stalwart of Holy Trinity Church in Chesterfield, its bible study class and sewing circle, as well as serving as Chairman of the Chesterfield Conservative Association. Her husband John, a successful iron and steel merchant, died quite young, long before I was born, so I always knew Ethel as a widow living alone in a four-bedroomed Victorian villa called Red Neuk on Newbold Road on the outskirts of Chesterfield. For many years she had had a live-in maid called Ivy, who had retired by the 1960s, so as Brown Grandma was getting older and frailer, three of her children – Jack, Rosemary and the youngest sibling, Jean – took it in turns to go to stay for the weekend to keep her company and attend to any urgent practical matters. Although the house was not particularly large, it had very substantial grounds, including an alley of greenhouses and a tennis court that had long since fallen into disrepair, a field with an air raid shelter in it and a paddock rented out to a local farmer where he kept an ill-tempered horse. There was no central heating at Red Neuk, which meant the house was very cold in winter; so, rather than use the spacious former dining room, with its glass cabinets filled with china ornaments, as well as a lovely old upright piano, which was totally out of tune, Ethel and her visitors spent most of the time in the second reception room, into which had been squeezed a large dining table, four chairs, a sofa, two armchairs, a glass-fronted bookcase and all the paraphernalia necessary to keep a good fire going. Ethel liked to listen to the radio, but she did not have a television, and in fact she spent most of her time reading, which endeared her to me. It is true that her choice of literature was not very wide. She had complete uniform editions of William Makepiece Thackeray and Stanley Weyman, as well as a pile of paperback novels by Georgette Heyer, and she systematically worked her way through these three authors, starting once again at the beginning when she got to the end.

There was an exquisite but disconcerting antique print of an engraving of the Prodigal Son by Dürer at the top of the staircase, whose wide wooden stairs creaked as one mounted them. A grandfather clock on the half-landing chimed the hours. Otherwise the house was hung with indifferent Victorian oil paintings of sea-scapes and country views. A tiled passage ran the length of the front of the house, from the kitchen at one end to a narrow room that served as a walk-in china cupboard at the other, in which was stored an enormous painted dinner service redolent of a much grander entertaining past. Some of the tiles in the passage were loose and clattered when anyone walked on them, while through the window that looked out onto a wide verandah shadows were cast by flapping creepers. There was no refrigerator in the kitchen at Red Neuk, but a step led down into a larder which did serve to keep food fresh except at the height of summer. I always slept in what had been the maid's room, which was over the kitchen; in the wardrobe there was a large box of black-edged cards and envelopes announcing the deaths and funerals of departed relatives and friends, which Brown Grandma had kept yet never referred to. At the other end of the upstairs corridor was a pink bedroom filled with fluffy, stuffed furniture that reminded me of a ladies' dressmaker's. That room was always spoken of as the nursery, which is what it originally was. Bizarrely, one day when I went exploring there I found a 1930s English edition of Hitler's *Mein Kampf* lying in the bottom of the wardrobe, but I hastily put it back and never mentioned that I had seen it.

Despite their consanguinity, the Bishops could not have been more different from the Fryers. Rosemary's brother Jack was a loveable, jovial fellow who had married an equally vivacious wife. They both enjoyed a drink and had produced two sons and two daughters who were equally high-spirited, making them a very jolly family. The younger son, Jeremy – nearly a decade older than me – was Harold's godson, but there was little interaction between Harold and the wider Bishop clan. Rosemary told me that her mother had been opposed to her marrying a markedly older man, though she had later become reconciled to the union. But the real problem was that both Rosemary and Harold hated her younger sister Jean with a quite extraordinary vehemence. This seemed partly to stem from the fact that Ethel was said to have helped Jean out financially early in her marriage to a rather handsome man who became a bank manager, but probably the falling-out had more to do with childhood disagreements. Rosemary had been very close to her elder sister Doreen when they were girls, and rather resented the arrival of their much younger sibling. While Rosemary was working as a nurse during the Second World War, Jean was a schoolgirl whose school had been evacuated to Chatsworth House, the Duke of Devonshire's palatial country residence, or so Rosemary claimed, suggesting that this had gone to Jean's head. Whatever the truth of that, they were not on speaking terms, but the arrangement by which Jack, Rosemary and Jean rotated their weekend duties at Brown Grandma's, with or without some member of their family in tow (though never Harold) conveniently meant that the two sisters never had to meet face to face. Doreen was of course out of the picture, having for many years been confined to an institution, where she died in 1967.

It only took an hour and a half to drive to Red Neuk from Eccles, taking a route that passed over the moors above Disley and on through Chapel-en-le-Frith. I loved the wild countryside up there, with its sweeping views, stone walls and woolly sheep, though Rosemary's insistence on smoking while she drove the Daimler often made me feel sick. I much preferred it when I went on my own, which happened increasingly frequently in the winter and spring of 1967-1968. I do not remember what reason Rosemary gave for not accompanying me on those occasions, but I loved the freedom of getting totally away from the Fryer household and manoeuvring the powerful car as it roared up the hills. Looking after Brown Grandma was simple, as during the week she had a daily help who always ensured that enough provisions were in stock, and towards the end of her life she had visits from a nurse, too. A gardener looked after the grounds or at least those visible from the house.

Friday evening would be spent quietly indoors at Red Neuk, talking or reading or listening to the radio, but on Saturday Brown Grandma would be taken for a run in the Peak District. Lunch was always at some smart hotel such as the Rutland Arms in Bakewell or the Peacock Inn in Rowsley. I especially liked the former, which until its refurbishment had a huge, high-ceilinged Regency dining room that had previously doubled as a ballroom. Jane Austen reputedly stayed at the Rutland Arms while writing *Pride and Prejudice*. Every time we went there, Brown Grandma would recount how the name Bakewell derived from the old English Baedeca's Spring. We often bought some of the local delicacy, Bakewell pudding, when visiting the little town, though I didn't think it a patch on Eccles cakes. Ethel Bishop was very proud of her Derbyshire lineage, of Chesterfield's crooked spire and the town's distinctive tomato flavoured sausages, none of which seemed to have any resonance for Rosemary. I was sad when the visits to Chesterfield stopped when Brown Grandma was taken into a nursing home, dying shortly afterwards in September 1968. I felt I had infinitely more in common with her than with any of the Fryers.

* * *

Even when I was studying hard for my 'A' levels it was impossible to ignore political developments on the Continent which were dominating the British broadsheet newspapers and the television news. In January 1968, Alexander Dubček was elected First Secretary of the Communist Party of Czechoslovakia and what was soon dubbed the Prague Spring began, as the Czech government instituted a series of economic and political reforms that would briefly make the country the freest part of the Soviet bloc. At No. 35, Harold was even prepared to set aside his 20-year grudge against

Czech glassmakers for failing to make him a bespoke cut-glass punch jug, cheering the Czechs on in their brave defiance of Moscow. However, he warned that the Russians would never allow the Czechs the sort of freedoms they were seeking and he predicted that the Dubček experiment would be crushed, recalling the way that the Hungarian Revolution had been snuffed out in 1956. I thought he was just being his grumpy old pessimist self, but events would prove him right.

Much closer to home, as well as being something that I felt concerned me personally more directly, were the May 68 events in France. They started as student occupations of university campuses as Marxist and socialist students, supported by some of their professors, protested against capitalism, materialism and the traditional French values of the family and the Catholic Church. It was also a generational struggle as young firebrands challenged older, middle-class voters who had kept the 77-year-old General Charles de Gaulle in power as President ever since the Fifth Republic that he had formed in 1958 came into being. Soon the students were joined by workers in their millions, complaining about low wages and poor factory conditions, with the result that France's industrial economy effectively ground to a halt. De Gaulle, who secretly fled to a French military camp in Germany for a brief period, ordered the police and army to act firmly against the demonstrators, and their strong-arm tactics prompted the more radical protestors to rip up the cobble stones that gave much of central Paris its charm and throw them at the police. Places I remembered so clearly from just a few months previously, having stopped off in Paris on my way home from the summer course in Tours, now appeared on the TV screen as being at the heart of a revolution that was starting to influence students and other young people elsewhere in the world. However, much to Harold's satisfaction that 'revolution' proved to be short-lived; law and order prevailed and de Gaulle's party won an increased majority in the National Assembly in the parliamentary elections that June.

* * *

Over the summer, Harold and Rosemary went to Canada and the north-west of the United States, having by now realised that they might as well use their abundant free time and money to see some of the rest of the world. I could have stayed on alone at No. 35, as I often would do in years to come, occupying Rosemary's bedroom so I could escape the ghosts that lingered in the room over the garage, but instead I persuaded my school-friend Roger to celebrate our finishing our 'A' levels by travelling to the very edge of Europe: Istanbul. The route I chose from the Encyclopaedia Britannica Atlas would take us down through the Netherlands, Germany, Austria, Yugoslavia and Bulgaria to Turkey, returning via Greece, Italy, Switzerland and France. Countless hours spent pouring over the Atlas as well as my growing stamp collection had ignited in me a determination to collect countries' border stamps in my passport as well, with the ultimate aim of visiting every country in the world, many of which were newly independent former European colonies. I had caused some amusement among officials in Luxembourg during a short school trip to the Low Countries some months previously by insisting that they stamp my passport as we entered the Grand Duchy from Belgium; in vain did they argue that border checks had long since been dropped between the three Benelux countries. Of course, this determination to add new countries to my collection was more than just a numbers game; my mind was like blotting paper, eager to soak up new experiences and new cultures.

In order to save money (which is the prime concern of most 18-year-old travellers) the idea was for Roger and I to hitch-hike for as much of the journey as possible, to stay in youth hostels and to buy most of our food from supermarkets, where these existed. We both had acquired khaki canvas rucksacks onto which had been sewn Union flags; someone had assured us that Britain's popularity just two decades after the end of the War was such that many drivers would stop to pick us up when they spotted the flags, which indeed did often prove to be the case. Moreover, few people were wary of hitch-hikers in those days, so by a rapid series of lifts on the first day, 28 June, three weeks after my 18th birthday, we reached Ware in Hertfordshire, where Hilary was by now living and teaching, in plenty of time to have tea and go 10-pin bowling. The following day we got to Harwich so quickly that we had to amble by the sea for several hours, watching the sailors walking out with their girls, before we could check in to the youth hostel. The next evening we boarded a cross-channel ferry, settling down in a twin-berth cabin with Horlicks and a cheese sandwich. Although we had both travelled to the Continent on school trips before, this was different: there were just the two of us and there were no grown-ups around who could tell us what we should or should not do.

* * *

The Customs officers at the Hook of Holland saw no reason to delay two British schoolboys or to delve deeply into our rucksacks, and a swift tram ride into the ultra-modern city of Rotterdam – largely rebuilt after the bomb damage from the War – set us on our way. The Union Jacks did their trick, as we were soon picked up as we headed for the motorway by a Dutch woman who had a horse in a trailer behind her car and who sang the praises of the British who had stood alone and defiant as the Germans overran Europe. The Common Market might have been in existence for over a decade – not that Britain was a member – but if the Dutch lady was anything to go by, resentment about the German occupation of Holland still went deep. Roger and I began to worry that maybe our flags might provoke a more negative reaction on the other side of the German frontier, but when we were dropped at a roundabout near Arnhem (and were dismayed to see a whole line of other hitch-hikers with their thumbs in the air), it was a German who picked us out of the queue and drove us over the border to Oberhausen, from where a tram and some buses got us to Essen.

The Schultz family, with whom I had stayed at Easter, had kindly suggested we stop off with them for a couple of days on our way down through Germany. The first evening we went to a cinema to see Louis de Funes in Le Petit Baigneux. The film was dubbed in German, which made Roger and I feel distinctly European, an identity we had already eagerly adopted despite the flags on our rucksacks; Europe was excitingly multilingual and enriched by centuries of vibrant continental culture. So different from dreary, monotone, monolingual England. The next morning Frau Schultz took us swimming at Essen's open-air Grugabad, but I was too shy to ask for vinegar to protect my skin and quickly got sunburnt. In the afternoon we cooled off in the adjacent park, where I gravitated to an enclosure that contained rabbits and guinea pigs. I still had a soft spot for small, furry creatures.

Frau Schultz handed us 20 Deutschmarks when she dropped us at the entrance to the Cologne motorway, which would be enough to feed us both for the next few days. Roger, who was already a firm Germanophile, was almost purring with contentment at the kindness we were receiving from the Germans, including the series of drivers that took us down in stages to Heidelberg. However, we had to laugh when we checked into the youth hostel in this handsome university town on the Rhine as it was run on almost military lines, making it almost a caricature of the prevailing British notion of German authoritarianism. At 9.30pm the Last Post sounded in the hostel and the lights were all turned out. A tannoy system ordered everyone not yet in bed to go upstairs to the dormitories immediately. But my giggles soon turned into groans of frustration at the snores of a young American in a nearby bunk kept me awake for most of the night. I was reminded of sharing a room with Harold in Mallorca, and pulled a pillow firmly over my head.

When we left the youth hostel the following morning, the 4th of July, Roger and I could not bring ourselves to wish the young American well for Independence Day, which US troops in Germany were celebrating. Although the American, British and French occupation of West Germany had officially ended in 1955, there was still a large American military presence in the area we were now passing through. Half the cars passing us as we stood by the side of the road waiting for a lift on the outskirts of Heidelberg were heading for Patrick Henry village, a large American installation complete with shops, schools, recreational facilities, churches and so on, and named after a renowned Governor of Virginia. If any Germans resented the continued American high visibility they were not showing it; most we spoke to were grateful that the Allied forces had stayed to guarantee West Germany's security, given East Germany's absorption into the Soviet bloc. Only five years earlier, President J.F.

Kennedy had made his famous 'Ich bin ein Berliner' speech to underline US and NATO support for the status of Berlin and West Berlin's links to the West following the East Germans' construction of the Berlin Wall, which was erected to prevent mass emigration to the West.

Heading down to Munich via Stuttgart proved easy; at one point we stood in the warm sunshine in an asparagus field, eating juicy cherries plucked from trees by the roadside. The last and longest ride was with a student in a Renault Deux Chevaux, who drove us right to the door of the Munich youth hostel. There, with the instant camaraderie that overland travel fosters in young people, we immediately fell in with a remarkably handsome but effeminate young Israeli guy who was accompanied by a chubby girl from New Zealand. She was making no secret of her desire to bed him. While humouring her, he was equally clearly not going to let it happen. These two kept crossing our path, separately or together, over the next few days that we spent in Munich, and I was astonished to hear from one of the other visitors at the youth hostel that the handsome Israeli was actually a gigolo, who made himself available to both women and men at the right price. It had never occurred to me that young men might sell sex as well as women; this left me fascinated and appalled in equal measure. I also wondered if sex could really be something so wonderful that even a woman would be prepared to pay for it.

While Roger and I were sitting on the outside steps of a supermarket where we had been stocking up on food for the long train journey we were about to take, a woman walked up to Roger and silently handed him a bar of chocolate. Maybe this was because he looked quite German with his blond hair or maybe because, unlike me, he looked as if he needed fattening up. Either way, as a good friend he shared this unexpected treat and it meant that we left both Munich and Germany with a sweet taste in our mouths.

* * *

The name Orient Express still had a romantic ring to it, though by 1968 the train was a pale shadow of its former self. When the

Compagnie Internationale des Wagons-Lits inaugurated its service from Paris to Constantinople, as Istanbul had long been known, it was a byword for luxurious travel, attracting the attention of many writers, not least Agatha Christie, whose *Murder on the Orient Express*, published in 1934, sealed in the public imagination the train's reputation for exoticism and international intrigue. It was also my favourite among all her books, which I had been devouring ever since neighbours in Eccles had given me paperback copies for the various garden parties. Indeed, the novel was probably the main reason I conceived the project of travelling to Istanbul, later persuading Roger to accompany me.

We joined the Orient Express at Munich's Hauptbahnhof, settling in to a six-seater second class compartment along with a young German couple and a Turkish migrant worker going home for a holiday from his job in Sweden. The seats were quite hard and the windows were dirty, and we were glad we had brought plenty of food and drink which we contributed to the compartment's kitty of shared meals over the next few days. At least the scenery through Salzburg and the Austrian Alps was beautiful, though I fell asleep before the train crossed into Yugoslavia.

We stopped long enough at Belgrade station for me to rush out to buy and write a postcard to send off to Hilary. Even if I was happy that Harold and Rosemary were over 5,000 miles away, out of sight and for the most part out of mind, I did not want to eject my adoptive sister from my consciousness. Back in the train, the German couple discovered that someone had stolen 260 Deutschmarks from their luggage. Meanwhile, as Roger and I stood in the corridor, two Turks offered us 200 Turkish lira and a hotel stay in Istanbul if we would take a tape recorder they had bought in Germany through the Turkish Customs, pretending it was ours, which was an offer we found easy to refuse. When the Bulgarian Customs officers came on board at the border with Yugoslavia they locked the compartment doors and went through everyone's luggage meticulously. The German couple, still smarting from the robbery, were annoyed when they were told sharply that they must pay 40 DM for visas, as they had not obtained one in advance. 'If you think the Bulgarian officials are bad,' our

Turkish travelling companion commented once the surly Customs men had left, 'you should try going to Romania!'

That night we were woken several times by immigration officials as the train left Bulgaria and briefly transited a narrow stretch of Greek territory before entering Turkey. It was already after 10 in the morning when the Orient Express slowly meandered through the Istanbul suburbs of four- and five-storey wooden houses, mostly dilapidated but very atmospheric, before disgorging us at the Serenci station, almost on the shore of the Bosphorus, where more Customs officers awaited, though Roger and I were quickly nodded through.

* * *

Istanbul in 1968 was a city of just two million souls, one sixth of its size today, and it was strikingly 'Oriental', despite the late Mustafa Kemal Ataturk's determination to Europeanise the new Republic of Turkey when it came into being in 1923. As soon as Roger and I emerged from the Serenci station we were accosted by men wanting to change money, or sell us donuts, water and fresh orange juice, or to clean our shoes. The youth hostel was just up the hill in Sultanahmet, right next door to Hagia Sophia and across a dusty square from the Blue Mosque.

That evening as we went for a stroll, keen to exercise our legs after several days on board the train, I soon realised that my shorts were creating a lot of unwanted attention from the men in the streets, which were almost devoid of women. We tried to sit down in a small garden near the Topkapi Palace but were shooed away from there by soldiers, which seemed to suggest it was a military area, so instead we found a bench opposite the mosque. Two Turkish men instantly came and sat next to us, and when one started stroking my bare thigh I realised we had better go back to the hostel to change. We returned to the bench once we had put on long trousers and for a while watched the local men walking arm in arms, some with a flower behind their ear, until one sat down next to Roger, patted the back of his neck and started to make a cooing noise like a pigeon. At that point we decided to call it a night.

108

We were up early the following morning to visit the Blue Mosque; in those days, one could just wander in, after removing one's shoes at the door, as was the case with Hagia Sophia. The Mosque was carpeted with hundreds of Oriental rugs and smelt strongly of stale socks. But the most striking thing, in every sense of the word, was the collection of grandfather clocks distributed around the prayer hall, so worshippers would know the time for prayer. At least in the mosque we were safe from wandering hands, but back out on the street the persistent attention started again, one young man trying to drag me into a taxi with him. Another wanted to sell us hashish. In the evening, Roger said he was feeling sick, so I went out instead with a young blond American who was also staying at the hostel, to visit the Bazaar. As the American was in his twenties and 6'5" tall, I thought we would be spared the amorous attentions of local men, but not a bit of it. The American thought this was very funny, but understandable in a society in which contact between the sexes prior to marriage was severely limited.

On the Saturday, Roger and I got a ferry over the Bosphorus to Üsküdar, as there were no bridges in those days. As I remembered from 'O' level history, Scutari, as the British historians called it, had been where Florence Nightingale ran her hospital for soldiers wounded in the Crimean War. Stepping foot on Asian soil for the first time was a tremendous sensation for me, even more significant than the sumptuous treasures we had enjoyed seeing in the Topkapi Palace museum the day before. We walked around the area near the jetty for a while, but Roger was still not feeling well and wanted to go back to the European side as soon as possible. As we were on the return ferry, I looked back over my shoulder until my neck ached, feeling like a child who has had a bag of sweets snatched from his hand.

* * *

When I stepped off the ferry and my right foot touched the ground, Asian soil, I felt an almost electric charge, a thrill nothing short of exhilaration. Ever since Mr Firth's class at Branwood House, nearly a decade ago, I have dreamed of being in Asia, the largest, most populous continent, home to such a rich diversity of peoples and civilizations. This is somewhere Harold has never been and probably never will visit. It is a place completely without his trace. I have proved that I can get here, and be here, and feel at home here.

Roger is my best friend. In fact, he is my only friend. But I don't mind that he doesn't feel the same excitement as me, or that he wants to get back to the safe familiarity of Europe.

I will be back here in Asia, and next time I will be sure to be alone.

Part Two

OUT

Because Turkey and Greece had recently been in conflict on several occasions and there had also been a coup d'état in Athens, in which a group of colonels seized power the year before Roger and I made our trip, Roger had insisted we do the Istanbul-Athens leg by air. Accordingly, we had bought flight tickets with BEA before we left England. However, the American at the Istanbul hostel said he would drive us to Athens for half the price, if we could cash in our tickets. Unfortunately that proved to be impossible, except back in the UK. This was frustrating as I would have liked to see the areas over which we would now have to fly, and as I complained to Roger, flying somehow seemed like cheating as part of an overland trip.

At Athens airport, Immigration officials checked our names against a typed list of undesirable aliens; the Colonel's coup and subsequent crackdown on civil liberties meant that NGO researchers as well as Western European journalists were trying hard to get into Greece to document what was happening and the Colonels were equally determined to stop them. Peter Benenson had founded Amnesty International only seven years previously and the Greek dictatorship was coming under a lot of scrutiny in Britain, but the Immigration clearly thought that two 18-year-old schoolboys with rucksacks offered little threat, as indeed was the case. But that did not stop me from being thrilled when we got a bus into town and saw our first army tank, parked in Omonia Square.

It was blisteringly hot in Athens, which meant that we spent most of our time lying exhausted on our bunks in the youth hostel, drinking chilled milk from a shop over the street, rather than visiting the sites (other than a quick jaunt up to the Acropolis), So after a couple of days we decided to head for the islands. For less than £1 each we got a ferry to Mykonos, where disembarking passengers were decanted by small motor boats. Although already discovered by discerning tourists, Mykonos was not yet commercialised and everything there was astonishingly cheap. We found a hostel in one of the whitewashed houses a short walk from the quayside and chose what would become a favourite café by the water's edge. Late every afternoon, the town's mascot, a Pelican called Petro, flew into the harbour and then wandered contentedly among islanders and visitors alike, looking for titbits.

It is really beautiful here and it is wonderful to feel quite happy for once. Travel seems to be like some mystical drug with me, driving away unpleasant thoughts about Eccles. Moreover I am convinced I need to write something; a novel, maybe. Already on this trip I have met people along the way who would make wonderful characters in a story, like the Israeli gigolo in Munich or the young British woman we met in Istanbul who had just survived a hair-raising journey by train from Baghdad with her infant daughter, or the half-Russian, half-German youth in Piraeus who told us he was heading for Afghanistan in search of cheap hash.

It's the Caerphilly by-election today; I can't see the Liberal doing much good. But Britain and its politics seem so far away. I'm sitting on the quayside, about to order another coffee. Petro the pelican has just strolled by.

* * *

Unfortunately, the ability to write anything more consequential than a diary while traveling was severely compromised, as Roger and I moved from place to place. We had decided to abandon the idea of visiting Italy, instead hitching northwards through Greece, but this proved to be very slow as there was little traffic and most drivers were unwilling to stop, so sometimes we had to catch local buses instead. Every time we passed a shrine all the passengers on the bus, along with the driver, would cross themselves, which was unnerving as the bus negotiated narrow bends. On a couple of occasions we had to stay in hotels, but as these cost no more than 12/6 (65p) this was an affordable luxury. I could see why Lawrence Durrell and other expat British writers had moved to Greece. It was so inexpensive, the food was fresh and tasty, and the weather, away from the summer furnace of Athens, was infinitely better than in England. Moreover, the local people were invariably friendly, often coming up to us and pressing fruit or bread into our hands as we stood by the roadside waiting for a lift. The fact that we had no common language in which to communicate was immaterial. The soldiers we met along our route were equally friendly, proffering cigarettes and chanting 'Manchester United!' when we told them where we were from.

Yugoslavia was to prove much more difficult and several times we had to resort to trains as no vehicles stopped. Belgrade, where we rested for a day, giving me the chance of getting a better idea of the city than I had gained from my brief dash from the train station to the post office on our way down through the Balkans, seemed horribly drab. It still bore many scars from the Second World War and the people looked care-worn and grey. Conditions improved as we headed towards Maribor in Slovenia. Subsequently, hitching through Austria was easy, but when we arrived in Munich during a violent thunderstorm we learned that the autobahn was closed due to flooding. That meant we had no choice but to get a train to Ostend via Cologne, hitching once again from the ferry terminal at Dover.

By the time we got near to Manchester, where Roger's parents picked us up from a phone box on an exit road from the M6, we were both tired after nearly six weeks on the road, and I was keen to learn my 'A' level results. These turned out to be straight As; my form master had scribbled on the postcard bearing the news 'Well Done!'; he was probably as surprised as I was. Soon there would be Hilary's wedding to her Welsh fiancé – who was also a PE teacher – at Monton Parish Church, near Worsley Golf Club, for which Harold and Rosemary returned from North America. The wedding went off without a hitch, but it was the calm before a storm.

*   *   *

Today, Tuesday 27 August 1968, is H's 67th birthday. Nearly two months without seeing him had lulled me into a false sense of security, but barely an hour after being in the house together I feel my heartbeat quickening and my anger rising. I'd snapped at him when Hilary and Clive left on their honeymoon and he had declared that he didn't consider Clive 'good enough' for her. It wasn't just that Clive is Welsh, but rather that H doesn't think he comes from the 'right' sort of family. I told him it was none of his business, if they love each other, and that what he really meant was that as far as he was concerned Clive was not good enough to be <u>his</u> son-in-law.

Later, H moaned that thanks to my excellent 'A'-level results I would probably have to stay on another year at MGS to sit the Oxbridge exams, which would probably lead to university, which would mean that he would have to support me for another few years. Finally, this lunchtime, after I had given him his birthday present and he just put it on one side, saying he would open it later, I cracked. I stormed out of the room, ran upstairs, stuffed some clothes into my rucksack, along with my passport and the few traveller's cheques remaining from the European trip, and left the house.

I caught the No. 54 bus into town, then a train to Liverpool. I am not sure where I am going, but I am heading West, and as far away from <u>him</u> as possible.

*   *   *

In the early 20th century, Liverpool was still the maritime gateway not only to much of the British Empire but also to the United States. An estimated nine million people sailed from its port between 1830 and 1930 in search of a better life. But by the late 1960s Liverpool and its docks were in a sad state of decline, yet this seemed to me to be the obvious place to head for. Once there, though, the possibilities for flight were extremely limited, so I took the one that was readily available: an overnight ferry to Dublin in the Republic of Ireland.

114

On the boat I got talking to a young traveller who told me about a bed and breakfast place in the suburbs of Dublin which charged only 10 shillings (50p) a night, so when we landed that is where I headed and unpacked my rucksack while I pondered my next move. America seemed the most promising option; after all, several million Irish had emigrated to the United States, going on to make a bright future for themselves despite arriving in New York with as little money as I had, or even less. So my first stop the following day was the American Embassy, which was housed in a striking new circular building on Elgin Road in Ballsbridge, so I could apply for a visa. Conveniently, I had some passport photos left from the European trip with Roger. However, the polite young consular official informed me that as a British citizen I could only apply for a visa in London, so that was that.

There seemed no point in hanging around in Dublin, so I hitched across the country to Galway, then on to Sligo and eventually back to Dublin, staying in youth hostels and trying to avoid the rain. The green, almost empty expanses of Eire's interior were impressive, though this was not the sort of landscape that enthralled me. By 4 September my money was starting to run out, so I returned to Manchester by the same route that had brought me to Ireland. Neither Harold nor Rosemary seemed curious about where I had been, or perturbed that I had just taken off without warning. I sensed this as a kind of victory, as it meant that I could now come and go as I pleased.

* * *

When I returned to Manchester Grammar to prepare for the Oxbridge entrance exams I had become one of the charmed group who could wear their own clothes and make coffee in the common room in the Sixth Form Block. I drew some money out from my Burnley Building Society account and bought a sports jacket from Kendal Milne's to celebrate. It was pale fawn and soft to the touch, rather like the golden retriever Tonya, and it had a gold silk lining; unfortunately I did not have enough money to buy the matching

115

trousers. This was the first jacket I had ever owned, apart from school blazers.

Because of my passion for maps and foreign travel I had decided that Geography would be my chosen subject at university, but the choice of Oxford, and St. Edmund Hall in particular, was entirely due to the influence of my favourite geography master at MGS, who had studied there himself. Teddy Hall, as I was told I must call the college, was one of the oldest and smallest in Oxford and it had a particularly strong reputation for Geography, many of whose students also played rugby or rowed for the college. Sports were clearly a high priority for many Teddy Hall men – and they were all men in those days – but I did not let that put me off the place when I went down to Oxford for an interview. The front quad was (and remains) beautiful, intimate in scale, without any of the pretentiousness of some of the bigger colleges, and the dons were friendly and welcoming. They discounted my total lack of interest in any sport when I told them about travelling overland to Istanbul and about my intention to go back to Asia before the beginning of Michaelmas term, 1969, if I passed the necessary exam and was admitted to the college. The fact that I was interested in politics and current affairs also went down well. When I returned to Eccles, I was buoyed by the feeling that Oxford was safely in the bag and that an escape route away from Harold lay ahead.

* * *

Just before I had bolted off to Ireland, the Soviet Union led Warsaw Pact troops in an invasion of Czechoslovakia, putting a brutal end to the Prague Spring, though Alexander Dubček remained nominal leader of the country for a few more months. The United States protested, but the Russians were correct in their assumption that America's growing entanglement in Vietnam would mean they had no appetite for anything beyond stern words in Central Europe. Harold was pleased to have been proved right about Soviet perfidy, but there was consternation at No. 35. Now fully bitten by the travel bug after his North American trip and eager to escape at least some of the English winter, Harold had booked himself and Rosemary plus me to go on a Christmas and New Year cruise to Iberia, Morocco and the Canary Islands on a Russian ship called the Aleksandr Pushkin. Given the Soviet invasion of Czechoslovakia, he wondered whether to cancel the cruise in protest, but as that would mean losing all the money he had paid for it, financial prudence prevailed, so he swallowed his political pride and decided we should go ahead as planned.

The Aleksandr Pushkin (subsequently renamed the Marco Polo after it was bought by Orient Lines in 1991) had been in service for just three years, initially for the Baltic Shipping Company, cruising round the Baltic Sea and in the summer running a service from Leningrad to New York via Helsinki and Tilbury. The 1968 Christmas cruise was a first for the ship, as it was for us; both the crew and the passengers were a little nervous when we set sail from Tilbury, given the political climate. Quite a lot of the passengers who had booked the holiday had indeed cancelled because of the invasion of Czechoslovakia, but there were some interesting characters among those who had decided to make the trip. Harold and Rosemary quickly found bridge partners, leaving me to my own devices. I shared a cabin with a middle-aged bachelor from Chiswick in West London, but saw little of him. When the ship docked at ports including Vigo, Casablanca and Las Palmas, most passengers piled onto coaches for shore excursions, while I marched off on foot in another direction – a practice I would continue many years later when I became a regular guest lecturer on cruise ships.

Most of the passengers were middle-aged or elderly couples, with whom I had little interaction, with the notable exceptions of the architect Philip Powell and his wife Philippa. Together with his practice partner Hidalgo Moya, Philip had designed the futuristic Skylon at the 1951 Festival of Britain as well as the Festival Theatre at Chichester, but despite his professional eminence he was a most unassuming man, short in stature, with a wry sense of humour and a permanent twinkle in his eye, whereas the taller, slender Philippa was gregarious to the point of being the soul of the party on board the Aleksandr Pushkin. This perplexed some of the Russian navy seamen who had been transformed into cruise stewards for two weeks and who had clearly never come across anyone quite like her.

117

She could not resist making jokes about Stalin, and thought it was hilarious that I came from Eccles, as that was her maiden name, which she pronounced in a voice imitating Peter Sellers in the BBC Home Service's Goon Show. She won my immediate affection by declaring about Harold, 'He looks positively *dire*, darling!'

There was only one other young person among the passengers, a girl from Lytham St. Anne's called Linda Shortland, who was slightly older than me and travelling with her parents. Inevitably we ended up dancing together when the band played music after dinner. I had learned most classical ballroom styles, as well as the cha-cha-cha, when I was sent for dance lessons at the age of about 13, when I had to partner the lady who ran the dance school in Monton; the teacher was so rotund I could not get my arms round her. In the interim I had been called on to dance with various ladies at functions, but I think Linda was the first girl I danced with other than my sister Hilary. More important, Linda had an impish sense of humour and a healthy disregard for adults, which meant that we found a lot to laugh about together.

While Harold and Rosemary were safely out of sight playing bridge I enjoyed the nightly entertainment on board the ship, after my solitary wanderings on shore. The shows were compered by a stout and jolly Russian woman, presumably also Soviet navy personnel, not old yet distinctly matronly, whom I shall call Galina. All of the crew had been carefully selected to ensure that none would defect during the journey, as the Russian ballet star Rudolf Nureyev had done while on tour in Britain only seven years previously. But Galina disarmed many of the passengers by announcing on the first night that she understood that many of us might have complex feelings because of recent events in Czechoslovakia. 'I know you do not always get the truth in the Western media,' she declared with a broad smile, 'but you must understand that it was important to restore order after revisionist forces were trying to overturn the victories of the Czechoslovak Communist Party.' At this point, Philip Powell rolled his eyes and Philippa stifled a laugh. 'Of course, you must ask questions!' Galina carried on bravely. 'On this ship, you are free to ask what you want!' As she looked round with a triumphant grin she knew that she had gauged the predominantly

118

British audience well, as no-one wanted to create a scene by asking awkward questions but instead just shifted a little uncomfortably in their seats.

Galina seemed to take an almost maternal interest in me, as she often saw me sitting on my own, when I was not in a huddle with Linda. So she was thrilled when I won the fancy dress competition on the final evening of the cruise as we sailed back to England. I went as Intourist, the Soviet state travel agency, having pinned onto my clothes numerous travel brochures about the Soviet Union. I went round the dance floor, which doubled as a stage, murmuring in a ham Russian accent, 'Do come to Russia! See what we have for you in Moscow!' When I was declared the winner, Galina beamed and asked me, 'and what would the young man like as a prize?'. But her expression changed rapidly when I replied, 'You!' I just meant as a friend, but she was furious and stomped off the stage in a rage. I may have been 18, but in my childlike innocence I still had not the remotest understanding why.

* * *

I had stopped writing my diary when I returned from the Irish jaunt, partly because there was nowhere I felt comfortable writing it at No. 35, but mainly because I had realised that Harold was going through my drawers and possessions while I was out of the house and I did not want him getting an insight into my inner thoughts. These were in fact increasingly political, as I no longer had much school homework to think about. I put a small ad in the Eccles Journal, two weeks running, asking for anyone interested in joining a new Young Liberal group to get in touch, but nobody responded. Despite this local setback, the National League of Young Liberals was enjoying considerable success elsewhere, much to the dismay of Jeremy Thorpe. Radical Young Liberals such as Peter Hain (later a Labour cabinet minister) and Louis Eakes (later Editor of Tribune) preached direct action rather than standard campaigning and put that into effect by demonstrating against the Vietnam War, South African sports tours and apartheid. With relish the popular Press dubbed the Young Liberals the 'Red Guards', equating them with the young

119

ideological foot-soldiers who were by now wreaking havoc in the Cultural Revolution in China.

However, some Young Liberals, especially in the North West, were more interested in combining radical idealism with what would become known as community politics. These activists included Gordon Lishman, later Director-General of Age Concern, who had recently graduated from Manchester University, and to whom I turned when I was in search of a mentor. Gordon was Chairman of the North West Young Liberal Federation and either by election or appointment – probably the latter – I became Vice-Chairman. The psephologist Michael Steed, who was Lecturer in Government at Manchester University as well as a regular pundit on TV election night programmes, was another contact who helped to point me in the right direction politically.

* * *

My main preoccupation nonetheless was planning how and when I would get away from Eccles during the months between leaving school and going up to Oxford. The concept of a 'gap year' had not yet gained wide currency, but I was determined to spend as long a period as far away as possible before I took up the Open Exhibition Award which I learned I had won at St. Edmund Hall. My initial scheme was to travel right round the Mediterranean, hitch-hiking as much as I could, down through France and Spain to Gibraltar, then across North Africa to Egypt and the Middle East, returning from Turkey via Greece and Italy. I reckoned that should be feasible during the three months or so that I would have available. But then I encountered a snag. Following the Six Day War between Israel and its Arab neighbours in 1967, Syria had broken off diplomatic relations with Britain, which it saw as a staunch ally of Israel. So there was no longer a Syrian embassy in London and no Syrian visa would be forthcoming for a British passport holder anywhere else. Annoyed at thus being thwarted I wrote a letter to then President, Nureddin al-Atassi, in Damascus, protesting that if his Ba'ath Socialist Party was such a champion of solidarity between peoples of the world then it was outrageous that a British schoolboy was prevented from visiting his country. I did not expect to get a reply, so once the letter had been posted I forgot all about it and started to work on Plan B.

During one of my long sessions in the library at MGS I had spotted an advertisement for a penfriend club called Les Amis du Courier, based in Spa in Belgium. This put mainly French-speaking teenagers around the world in touch with each other. This seemed an attractive proposition, as well as giving me a chance to practise my French, so I signed up and acquired a number of pen-pals, notably a girl in Nhatrang in South Vietnam and a boy in Phnom Penh, Cambodia, both in former French Indo-China. The letters were soon flying back and forth, even if they sometimes took several weeks to arrive, and in January 1969, Cham, the Vietnamese girl, wrote to say that as my Mediterranean plans had evaporated, why did I not come to visit her in Vietnam? It was true that I was keen to know more about the Vietnam War, against which the Young Liberals were so vocal. I was not sure what to think about it myself. The Americans claimed it was necessary to prevent a Communist takeover of the country which, according to their Domino Theory, would otherwise put the rest of Indo-China, then Malaysia and Singapore, Indonesia and eventually Australia in danger from the Reds. This argument seemed to have a certain logic to it, yet already disconcerting reports were emerging of the effect of the War on the lives of ordinary Vietnamese and the country's environment.

Cham's family were Roman Catholics and her father was a former government employee who had taken early retirement; they were fearful what would happen to them if the Communists ever succeeded in taking over the South. It was thanks to Cham's letters that my Plan B crystalised: to go to Vietnam to find out about the War for myself. I was still determined to travel overland as far as was possible, which would clearly require more than the three months that I had envisaged. That meant I would have to get permission from MGS to leave school early. In principle the school was opposed to this, as it meant they would not qualify for the government grant they could claim for me that year. I therefore had to go to see the High Master, Peter Mason, for the first time since the disastrous afternoon Harold had taken me to play for Lawrence

Leonard at the Free Trade Hall. Mr Mason was surprisingly amenable; I guess he was impressed by the initiative, though at the time I suspected MGS was glad to see the back of me. If so, the feeling was mutual. I did not set foot again there for almost half a century.

Of course I needed to work out how to pay for this long trip across Asia. One of the Manchester Liberals suggested I ask the party nationally if they had any short-term paid post which would supplement my meagre savings in the Burnley Building Society account, and so it was arranged that I should go down to London to meet the Head of the Liberal Party Organisation, Pratap Chitnis. Through a friend of a friend of one of the Manchester Liberals, I was offered a place to stay for the night in London, once I had hitched there. To take up this offer when I arrived in the capital I had to go to one of the big department stores in Oxford Street, where my host worked in the handbag department. Once he had finished work, we caught a bus to his home in South London, where after a light supper we went to his freezing bedroom. There we squeezed chastely into his single bed. Above this hung a photograph of Pierre Trudeau, who had been elected Liberal Prime Minister of Canada the year before, and whom my host claimed proudly to have bedded.

The meeting with Pratap Chitnis the following morning at the LPO's offices in a tiny courtyard off The Strand went better than I dared hope. By chance, the Labour MP for the inner-city Birmingham parliamentary seat of Ladywood, Victor Yates, had just died, and although this would not normally have been considered fertile territory for the Liberals, Pratap Chitnis – who had master-minded Eric Lubbock's successful campaign in the sensational Orpington by-election in 1962 – believed that the Party did have a chance in Birmingham Ladywood. The constituency was compact and had a very small electorate, because of recent slum clearance. Moreover, a populist local Liberal councillor called Wallace Lawler was getting a lot of national as well as local publicity for his shaming of Harold Wilson's government for allegedly not doing enough to address the problems of inner-city housing and poverty. Wallace Lawler was duly selected as the by-election candidate and Pratap Chitnis said that if I could go to Birmingham at short notice he would find some money to make me a sub-agent, to help set up the campaign under the guidance of a party employee already in place in the city.

The arrangement with the Birmingham Liberals was that I would go there for a period of six weeks, including Easter. I would be paid a modest fee and would be put up by a couple of local activists in their home in the suburb of Rednal. This meant that every morning I had to commute into central Birmingham on a slow-moving double-decker bus, past the Cadbury's Bourneville Estate and the Longbridge car works. It reminded me of the journey through Salford from Eccles to MGS, except that in this case there was nothing to dread at either end.

The Birmingham Liberal HQ was rather old-fashioned and totally devoid of the sort of sophisticated equipment and mountains of leaflets that one finds in a by-election headquarters today. As I could type, I was put in charge of a massive typewriter, in front of which I sat for much of the day, answering queries that were coming in from Ladywood and beyond. There was a series of standard responses to easy enquiries – all of which nonetheless had to be typed out individually – but for more complex issues I had to consult the candidate, usually in the living room of his neat, comfortable house. Some people found Wallace a little overbearing and far too right-wing on a number of political issues, but he was always helpful and understanding with me, avuncular even. On the rare occasions I was allowed to go out canvassing with him I was amazed by his rapport with the inhabitants of what was one of the most run-down areas of the city. Everyone seemed to know him and to know about the things he was doing for the local community, so I was not at all surprised to learn the day after the election that was finally held on 26 June – by which time I was in Vietnam – that he had won, garnering over 50 per cent of the vote.

My host family in Rednal could not have been more hospitable, even cooking me a full English breakfast, something that had never happened at No. 35. Moreover, they went away on a long-planned holiday over Easter, leaving me in the house on my own. One evening, after a long but particularly fruitful day at the office, I put a record of Ravel's Bolero on the stereo in their large living-room and danced alone around the room with ever increasing intensity until the music came to an end.

* * *

Though I had managed to save almost all the modest fee the LPO gave me, that was only a drop in the ocean compared with what I would need for six months in Asia, but I planned the fund-raising with the same degree of care as I had used when organising the garden parties in the past. Emboldened by my early journalistic efforts in the Mancunian, the school newspaper, I rang the recently appointed Editor of the Manchester Evening News, Brian Redhead (with whom I would years later coincide on BBC Radio 4's Today programme) and told him that I had left MGS early in order to go to Vietnam and to ask if he would commission some articles from me. Far from dissuading me, as many in his position would have done, he was enthusiastic and although he could not guarantee that the Evening News would publish what I filed, if they liked it and used it then I would be paid the normal freelance rate. True to his word, he then got his secretary to type out a letter of accreditation.

Armed with the letter from the Manchester Evening News it was then easy to get further commissions 'on spec' from other publications, notably the Geographical Magazine. The ever-faithful Eccles Journal wrote a long story about my proposed adventure, though they spiced it up into a human interest feature by suggesting that my main motive was a romantic one, to meet up with my penfriend Cham. That story was picked up by both the Daily Mail and the Daily Telegraph, causing Harold to emit a rare grunt of approval. I began to see a vibrant freelance journalistic career rolling out in front of me. But naturally no money would materialise from these potential articles, even if the pieces were accepted, until well after I was planning to leave. The only option therefore was to try to persuade Harold to put the money up front.

The argument I used was that as he had given Hilary an Austin Mini for her 21st birthday (of which to his fury she later disposed, in part exchange for a second-hand Rover that had previously belonged to the Lord Mayor of Oxford) he ought to consider giving me the same amount of money as the Mini had cost (about £600, or £9,300 in 2016 terms) in lieu of a 21st birthday present two years hence. It must have been the fact that I had effectively clinched some media assignments that made him agree. Or maybe he was just pleased to see the back of me. Neither he nor Rosemary ever uttered a word of concern about my heading off into a war zone. Usefully, Harold did say that I could borrow his camera, which he had hardly used, except on holiday, providing I wrote regular bulletins home about what I had been doing, which seemed a fair bargain.

* * *

As I had no suitcase of my own, I was allowed to take one of the brown leather suitcases usually employed to transfer the silver to the Bank, as well as a smaller blue case that Hilary had left behind at No.35. It seemed odd not to be travelling with a rucksack for once, but that would probably have given people the wrong impression. I packed far too much, including a sizeable medical kit, and when the leather suitcase fell apart almost as soon as I hit the tropics, with relief I dumped it and most of its contents, travelling the rest of the way with just the small blue case and a minimum of clothing.

My ultimate destination had to be kept a secret from fellow travellers when I set out on 28 April with visas in my passport for East Germany, Poland and the Soviet Union and a ticket bought through Intourist that would take me all the way from London to Yokohama in Japan. I joined the train to Moscow in Brussels and was woken several times that night by immigration officials and ticket inspectors as we crossed from West Germany into East Germany, then from the DDR into West Berlin, then on to East Berlin and the DDR once more. Each stop involved passport controls and rigorous checks by the East German border guards. Later, at Bialystok on the Polish frontier with Soviet Belarus, all the passengers had to disembark while the carriages were lifted off the track before being lowered again onto the wider Russian bogeys. The coaches were provided by the West German rail company, Deutsche Bahn, so were reasonably comfortable, though there was no restaurant car for second class passengers. Accordingly we bought food and drink through the windows from vendors on station platforms where the train stopped, the Deutschmark being the main currency in demand.

At Moscow I was met by a man from Intourist who drove me in his little Lada to the Hotel Ukraina on the south bank of the Moskva River. When I arrived at reception I said there must be some mistake, as I was travelling second class and this was clearly one of Moscow's finest hotels, even in Soviet days. But the stony-faced woman behind the desk would not permit herself to admit that Intourist could make a mistake, so instead she took my thick booklet of vouchers – which included coupons for the Moscow hotel, the Trans-Siberian railway and all meals en route – and ceremoniously ripped out the breakfast voucher for the following morning which she then tore into pieces, declaring triumphantly, 'No breakfast!'

At least I had a free evening to look round Central Moscow. It was chilly but the snow had melted and opposite the GUM department store in Red Square preparations were being made for the May Day parade. The Hotel Ukraina itself – these days refurbished and rebranded the Raddison Royal – was a fine example of Stalinist neo-classical architecture and only 12 years old, though it felt older. The wide avenue in front of the hotel was almost devoid of traffic, except for the Zil limousines of high Soviet officials which raced down the central lane reserved exclusively for their use, making me think of the classic line in George Orwell's *Animal Farm*: 'all animals are equal, but some animals are more equal than others'. I imagined Guy Burgess, the most notorious of the so-called Cambridge spies, who had died in Moscow only six years previously, walking down these streets, and I wondered if his cohort Donald McLean was still around. It was not unnatural to think of espionage, as the Cold War was still very much in force. Despite the reforms of the late Nikita Krushchev and the occasional expressions of friendship between peoples, suspicion between Britain and the Soviet Union was mutual and deep.

* * *

In keeping with the Soviet Union's Communist ideology, the Trans-Siberian railway did not have first and second class carriages, but instead 'soft' and 'hard', which was in fact an accurate description of the respective sleeping berths. I shared a 4-person couchette cabin with a young Swedish couple from Uppsala, while in the adjoining carriage of 'soft' berths there were a few Americans, notably a tall, gangly, middle-aged insurance and tax consultant from Louisville, Kentucky, named John Moyse. John liked to portray himself as a die-hard conservative who ate liberals for breakfast and he proved to be an entertaining traveling companion over the next 12 days by keeping up a running commentary on the supposed perfections of the Soviet system. The foreigners on the train were deliberately grouped together, but Russian passengers had to pass through our carriages in order to get to the dining car. Most went by as fast as they could, avoiding eye contact, as if they had been warned not to fraternise; but there was one marked exception: an anonymous-looking little man of about 40, who always wore a drab, mud-coloured jacket which had a small metal badge of a pair of boxing gloves pinned to one lapel. He frequently lingered in the corridor of both the carriages in which there were foreign travellers and he tried to engage us in conversation; though heavily-accented his English was quite reasonable. John Moyse and I quickly came to the same conclusion, that this non-descript fellow was in fact a KGB agent who was trying to find out as much about us as possible, maybe even to provoke us into saying something that could potentially get us into trouble or make us possible candidates for blackmail. We had both read about honeypot traps and other methods used by the Russians to compromise foreigners while they were in the Soviet Union.

I had already decided not to let on to anyone that I spoke some Russian and moreover I did not write a journal for that part of the journey, as I had been warned that our possessions would be searched while we were all having meals in the dining car, which indeed proved to be the case. The plump stewardess, who every so often brought us tea from the samovar at the end of the carriage, otherwise spent most of her time sitting in her little cabin with the door open monitoring everyone going past.

127

Once we were beyond the Urals the weather became distinctly colder and there was still snow on the ground. When the train stopped at stations, the stewardess would announce how long it was going to stay there and if the halt was more than ten minutes the Swedish couple and I, along with John Moyse and a few others, would alight so we could walk briskly up and down the platform to get some exercise. The exercise was part of an ultimately failed attempt to stave off constipation. Long hours of sitting on one of the hard lower couchettes, staring out of the window at bleak snow-covered expanses or reading, in English translation, Mikhail Sholokhov's *And Quiet Flows the* Don, did not facilitate bowel movement – a situation that was made worse by the fact that after the first couple of days the only food available in the dining-car at both lunch and dinner was tough steak with a fried egg on top. At least there was always good Russian beer. Sometimes I missed meals because of confusion over the time. Russia has no fewer than 11 time zones, which meant that we kept 'gaining' an hour as the train moved steadily eastwards, yet the trains themselves ran on Moscow time all the way across – another example of Soviet logic that kept us Westerners scratching our heads.

At stops in the middle of the Siberian countryside the train would be besieged by locals trying to persuade the catering staff who ran the dining-car to sell them food. In some of the larger towns and cities like Omsk and Tomsk there were cafeterias on the platform and we would ask permission to go in; embarrassingly, that was only possible if any Russian customers already in there were thrown out, which they seemed to accept as normal, despite quiet grunts of discontent.

After a few days the little KGB man was starting to get desperate as he had nothing particularly useful to report back to Moscow. His early questions to me had been inconsequential, such as asking which football team I supported; in such circumstances I always said Manchester United, even though I did not care a fig about the sport or any team. But by the time the Trans-Siberian was creeping very slowly along somewhat unstable rails round the bottom of the frozen Lake Baikal and I was staring out of one of the windows in the corridor at a group of fishermen wrapped up in furs out on the ice, he suddenly came up to me and said, 'Things are much better in England than in Russia, aren't they?' It was a leading question heading in a direction I had no intention to follow. John Moyse, in contrast, loved to tease the little Comrade, as John always called him. He feigned admiration for Josef Stalin as someone who 'knew what to do with lily-livered pinkos', unlike subsequent Soviet leaders.

Because Vladivostock, the final destination of our Trans-Siberian train, was a closed port to foreigners on security grounds, our little band of Western travellers was decanted one morning at Khabarovsk. There were several hours to kill there before a connecting train to the port of Nakhodka would arrive, but there was no question of our being allowed to wander freely round the city, as we would have liked. Instead, we were shepherded onto a coach, along with our luggage, and driven around town. The only place we were allowed to get off was at the Dinamo city leisure park, which is probably delightful in summer, with its wide array of sporting facilities for both adults and children, but it was deserted and looked miserable under ice and slush as winter was coming to an end. We jumped around a bit, thrashing our arms against our chests, to try to get warm before demanding to be let back on the bus.

The journey down from Khabarovsk to Nakhodka ran alongside the Ussuri River, which was just over the border from China. There had been clashes between Russian and Chinese troops in this region only a few weeks earlier, when People's Liberation Army troops had attacked Soviet border guards on the island of Zhenbao and seized a Russian tank. There were numerous Soviet casualties on that occasion, including 59 dead, and there were real fears that the situation could escalate into open warfare between the two Communist giants. So for the night-time part of this journey we travelled in total darkness as the Russians were worried the lights of a moving train might prove to be an irresistible target to the Chinese. One or two of the Americans were rather disconcerted by this development and wondered aloud whether we had been wise in taking the Trans-Siberian, but John Moyse and I were in our element, staring out of a window in the direction of China in the hope we might see something, but it was all pitch black.

John's crowning moment came on the Russian ship that took us from Nakhodka to Yokohama in Japan. At the aft of the main deck there was a giant chess-board marked out, with waist-high chess pieces made out of wood. John's eyes lit up and when an English-speaking Soviet naval officer was in earshot he declared with glee, 'Of course, in Tsarist days, they used serfs as pawns, and each time one was captured during the game he was thrown overboard!'

* * *

When we docked in Japan, most of the soft class passengers headed off to their respective hotels in Tokyo. John Moyse was annoyed that Frank Lloyd Wright's Imperial Hotel, near the Emperor's Palace, had been demolished just the year before; despite his mask as a crusty conservative, he liked modernist architecture. I made my way to a Japanese *ryokan* in the capital city: an inexpensive traditional inn, where one slept on the floor on a *tatami* mat, and had communal baths with other men in a pool whose water seemed to be barely below boiling point. Through sign-language, Japanese male guests in the bathhouse, who could not resist casting sideways glances at my large white body to see if we all belonged to the same species, indicated that one should wash with soap and small bowls of tepid water before going into the steaming bath for a soak. After the initial shock this hot-tub was marvellously relaxing and I could almost feel the pores of skin opening up to breathe. Unfortunately, the night was a much less pleasant experience, as I woke up in the early hours sneezing and wheezing. When the lady who ran the *ryokan* brought in my seaweed breakfast the following morning she was alarmed, but I knew exactly what the problem was: I was allergic to the *tatami* mats on the floor. As she spoke no English and I spoke no Japanese this was impossible to explain; I pointed to the floor and sneezed and she just laughed in embarrassment behind her sleeve. However, she took me off to see her doctor nearby. He was equally monolingual and bewildered as I talked about hay-fever and asthma, but then I said the word 'allergy' and his face it up. 'Ah, *arerugi*!' he declared, with a broad smile of relief. He prescribed some antihistamines, and the symptoms soon abated.

130

I was going to have to get used to sleeping on hard *tatami* mats, despite my itching nose and runny eyes, but most importantly the lesson was driven in to me that knowing English, French, German and some Russian just wasn't enough when one stepped beyond Europe. I would have to try to come to grips with Japanese and maybe other languages if I was going to spend any extended period of time in this part of the world. The fact that Japanese was written in a mixture of Chinese characters and two separate phonetic alphabets did make that prospect a little daunting. But it seemed that virtually nobody spoke more than a few words of English in Japan, despite two decades of US occupation. Nonetheless, as a young Westerner, if one sat down on a bench in a park, a Japanese schoolgirl would invariably sit next to you and say 'Hello!', which sounded more like 'Herro!', and then burst into a fit of giggles, but they were incapable of enunciating much else. The schoolboys, with their buzz-cut hair and military-style school uniforms buttoned up to the neck were more aloof, looking at one from the side of their eye as they marched round in groups, keeping their distance.

I stayed in Tokyo long enough to get my passport annulled and a new one issued at the British Embassy, as there was no way I would be able to travel to South Vietnam – or even Taiwan – with Communist visas in my passport. I then had to go to the immigration department in Yokohama to get a fresh Japanese entry stamp put in the new passport, before catching the bullet train down to Osaka. This was so much faster than anything we had in Europe, though it was frustrating that one could not really appreciate the scenery as we sped through the countryside. From then on I took things much more sedately, thanks to a series of local trains and buses, visiting Kyoto and Nara – two centres boasting magnificent temples and gardens – before taking a boat from Kobe to the island of Kyushu. In the hot-tub of a *ryokan* in the hot springs spa town of Beppu I got talking to a Japanese student of about my age who hailed from Okinawa and did speak more than a smattering of English. He explained that his father was one of Japan's greatest experts on Shakespeare and that if I would like to go to stay for a few days with his family in Okinawa, as I made my way south, I would be very welcome. Accordingly, we travelled together by ship to the Ryukyu Islands, of which Okinawa

131

was the most important. On arrival at Okinawa I was delighted to receive a separate stamp in my passport from the Ryukyu Governate; at that time the islands were still under American occupation – as they had been since the end of the Second World War – and they would only be returned to Japanese control three years later.

Okinawa is semi-tropical and is still the site of the principal US military bases in Japan. Around those bases in the Spring of 1969 one found the sort of small businesses and girlie bars that sprang up like toadstools everywhere near US military facilities in East Asia. My host family's house was a single-storey building arranged round a central garden of lush green vegetation, though my new friend urged me not to go out into the garden, as it was infested with poisonous snakes. His mother served us our meals in silence, as we sat with our legs crossed under a low table fixed above a shallow sunken pit. The father of the house never joined us, though occasionally I caught sight of him in traditional dress walking around his study on the other side of the garden. His son told me his father was extremely busy, but on the last day he confessed that the truth was that his father was too embarrassed to meet me. Although he was one of the leading Japanese Shakespeare scholars he was incapable of holding a conversation in English.

* * *

After leaving Okinawa, a series of boats took me down past the southern Ryuku Islands to Taiwan, where Chiang Kai-shek was still in charge. His Republic of China also retained China's seat at the United Nations, though they would lose that accreditation two years later following President Richard Nixon's historic visit to the mainland. Taiwan's capital, Taipei, was far poorer and less developed than Tokyo, for example, which undermined the credibility of my former primary school headmaster Mr Firth's claim that one day Chiang Kai-shek would return victorious to the mainland. It was probably only because Taiwan enjoyed such huge support from the United States that a forcible reunification of China had not taken place, though Communist China was by now going through the trauma of the Cultural Revolution, in which even some

132

senior party cadres as well as traditionally respected figures of authority in society such as university professors and artists were feeling the brunt of the Red Guards' violent hysteria. Since 1966, the People's Republic had been isolated internationally having repudiated its earlier brotherly relationship with the Soviet Union, and it had turned in on itself like a dragon eating its own tail.

The impact of the Cultural Revolution was even evident in the British colony of Hong Kong, as I discovered when I arrived there. Waves of refugees from the Chinese mainland had been swelling the colony's population ever since the declaration of the People's Republic on 1 October 1949, and now this included formerly loyal Communist officials who were fearful for their own future. But there were also demonstrations in the British colony by pro-Beijing activists and although I could not read the graffiti that had appeared in various parts of Hong Kong Island and the New Territories I was told that they reflected political struggles over the border. That border itself was firmly shut, as far as Western visitors were concerned, which helped give Hong Kong a claustrophobic atmosphere, heightened by the fact that so many people – nearly four million by then – were crammed into such a small area of land on both sides of the main harbour. I found accommodation on the island not far from the Star Ferry terminal in a hostel run by a middle-aged Australian and his Malaysian-Chinese wife on one of the upper floors of a building on Harbour Road. This had presumably once been an apartment block, but the lower floors were now being used by a series of workshops producing cheap manufactured goods; the racket from the machines during the day time was a good incentive for one to be out exploring the streets. The Australian and his wife had converted what would have been their apartment's living room into a dormitory, into which eight two-tier bunk beds had been squeezed, the middle two rows pushed together.

I never saw what must have been the proprietors' bedroom and kitchen at the back of the apartment, as these was out of bounds to the predominantly Australian backpackers who were the hostel's main guests. There was a loo which we could use, but the only washing facilities were provided by a single small white basin at one end of the dormitory, in which one also had to wash one's shirts and underwear. The weather was already quite hot and sticky, with high humidity, but a breeze did sometimes blow in through the open slats of the window blinds. The best bunks were the ones nearest the window, though those were also the ones onto which flying cockroaches sometimes landed. At least the accommodation was cheap. So too were some of the modest restaurants nearby that were patronised by the workers from the sweatshops in the building. One offered a bowl of nourishing soup of noodles with vegetables and tofu for just one Hong Kong dollar (less than 10p).

One evening, having got a visa from the Portuguese consulate in Hong Kong, I took an overnight ferry over to the Portuguese colony of Macau, which was very much a sleepy backwater in 1969, unlike the high-rise Oriental equivalent of Las Vegas that it is today. Red-and-white single-decker buses ran along half empty roads that were lined with trees and pastel-shaded Portuguese villas, many of which were starting to fall into ruin. The Portuguese were still trying to hold on to all of their Empire, unlike the British and the French, though their focus was more on the resource-rich colonies in Africa than on this obscure Asian outpost. I walked up to Macau's frontier with China, which was little more than a pole over the road, though soldiers on both sides made it clear I should not get too close. It would have been very simple for the Communist Chinese to occupy Macau, but they found it more useful to keep it as a back door to the outside world. I would have loved to have travelled into China and from there on to North Vietnam overland, but that was impossible. The only direct way to get to Vietnam was to take an Air France flight from Hong Kong to Saigon, as Ho Chi Minh City was still called.

* * *

Looking back, it seems strange that I felt no trepidation at the thought of flying into a war zone, but I genuinely had no sense of danger. Moreover, my first impression of Vietnam from the air was how closely the Saigon delta and its dendritic drainage system resembled textbook illustrations from my 'A'-level Geography textbooks. Then suddenly as the Air France jet descended to

Saigon's Tan Son Nhut airport one saw huge lines of American and Vietnamese military aircraft of every kind: B-52 bombers, transport planes, fighter jets, helicopters and so on. I could now credit reports that I had heard that Tan Son Nhut was the busiest airport in the world, based on the number of flights going in and out. Almost 550,000 American troops were stationed in the country, many of them conscripts of around the same age as me.

The arrivals terminal at the airport was small and dilapidated and it took an hour to get to the front of the immigration queue through a zigzag or wooden railings. My visa (acquired in Hong Kong, on presentation of my letter of accreditation from the Manchester Evening News) was in order, though it was only valid for two weeks, which is all the consulate would give me, telling me I must apply for an extension when I arrived in Vietnam. However, when I emerged with my luggage from the arrivals hall there was no sign of Cham, who had said she would come down from Nhatrang to meet me. I hung around for a while, feeling rather dejected, with a small black plastic YMCA sports bag slung over my shoulder, wondering what on earth I should do next. Then a tall, slender and self-evidently British man in his mid-30s came up to me and asked if I was alright. He introduced himself as Michael Counsell, Anglican Vicar of Vietnam and Cambodia; he had been seeing off a friend going to Singapore on the plane I had just arrived on, thoughtfully waiting until the plane had safely taken off. I explained that I had expected my Vietnamese penfriend to be there to meet me but that she had not materialised, and that I was now thinking of going into Saigon to see if by any chance she had left a message at the Air France office in town. He replied that if I needed accommodation for a few days, I would be welcome to stay at the vicarage, as his wife was back in England having a baby.

Michael Counsell's first experience of the Far East had been during his National Service, when he was posted to Hong Kong. On his return to Britain he was ordained as a Church of England priest and he then opted to go to Singapore as a missionary. For a short while he was a parish priest there until the Bishop of Singapore decided that he would be just the man to go as Priest in Charge of what was still often referred to as Indo-China, being young, fit, adventurous and resourceful. He was about half-way through his five year posting in Saigon when I met him. A talented linguist, he used the opportunity of a subsequent posting as Dean of St. Paul's Cathedral in the Seychelles to translate the four Christian Gospels into Seychellois creole.

The vicarage was a modest but comfortable 2-bedroom French villa in a cul-de-sac off Cong Ly, roughly half way between the airport and the city centre. That was indeed where I stayed for a while. I slept surprisingly well in the guest-room despite the fact that often at night the B52 bombers carpet-bombed a doughnut round the city, to prevent Viet Cong infiltration. Only the previous year, 70,000 North Vietnamese and Viet Cong troops had launched what became known as the Tet Offensive against towns and cities across South Vietnam during the traditional New Year holiday, temporarily taking control of the historic city of Hue and getting close to Saigon itself. During 1968, more than 15,000 US troops had been killed, but in response to the Viet Cong surge, General William Westmoreland, Commander in Chief of the US forces in Vietnam 1964-1968, asked for 200,000 extra soldiers to launch a counter-offensive. President Lyndon Johnson meanwhile ordered a halt to the bombing of much of North Vietnam and started to put out feelers for a negotiated settlement to the conflict. In retrospect, this was the beginning of the end of the US presence in Vietnam, though we were unaware of that at the time.

One of the legacies that the French had left behind since their time in charge of Indo-China was a bloated bureaucracy, which meant that my first days in Vietnam were spent filling in forms and supplying photographs, to get the necessary press accreditation, first from the Vietnamese authorities and then from the US military. The latter issued among other things an American press card and a MAC-V ID card, which would enable me to use US military canteens and stores and give me free travel on any American plane, military or civilian, going anywhere I wanted inside South Vietnam, providing there was room and there was time to get me on the manifest. That included the CIA's own airline, Air America, which carried not just spooks but civilian contractors, Peace Corps volunteers and the like. The precious card itself, bearing my thumbprint as well as a photo, was laminated, which was a process I had never seen before, and written on the back, in both English and Vietnamese, was a statement along the lines of: 'If captured, the holder of this card should be accorded the treatment due to a US Army Major'. I couldn't help thinking that if I were captured by the Viet Cong, the last thing I would want to be treated like was as a US Major. Chilling reports of how American POWs were mistreated in North Vietnam were already common currency. I deliberately did not cut my hair, so I would look as un-military as possible, and I tended to walk round Saigon with a copy of Paris Match under my arm, in the hope of appearing French, rather than American, in the belief that would be the lesser of two evils. However, the US ID card did prove invaluable for getting me round the country and at that stage in the War the Americans were keen to show foreign journalists exactly what they were doing, as they were so sure what they were doing was right. That was a mistake they would never make in a war situation again.

* * *

The streets in Saigon are full of hundreds of Honda motor-bikes, pedicabs and ancient French taxis. Everybody seems in a rush. There are plenty of soldiers and sandbags, but nobody takes much notice of either. After a while you almost get used to war and settle down to living as normal a life as possible. Saigon used to be known as the Pearl of the Orient, with its fine tree-lined boulevards, but it is a somewhat jaded pearl now. There are miles of barbed wire and horrifying air pollution from all the motor-cycles and bad petrol.

The floating restaurant on the Saigon River is still popular, despite frequent attacks by the Viet Cong. The main street, Tu Do, has been transformed by the emergence of girlie-bars catering for the American troops. The early afternoon is quiet, as people rest after lunch. During the monsoon season it is oppressively hot and sticky. The humidity rises steadily and at about 4.30pm there is usually torrential rain.

Vietnamese soldiers standing guard on street corners look bored and uncomfortable in their heavy uniforms. They frequently smile at white people or ask in sign language for a cigarette. Civilians, on the other hand, deliberately ignore you, though a few express some signs of contempt. If you are white you are assumed to be American and there is no way of getting out of paying twice as much as the Vietnamese do for taxis. There is a definite felling of 'us' and 'them', with an even more sinister 'them' lurking somewhere, ready to attack.

The one oasis in the city is a park where suddenly the angry buzz of the motor-cycles is silenced. There is a neatly-kept zoo where families linger as parents identify animals for their children, while along the alley-ways off-duty Vietnamese soldiers and sailors walk round in pairs, innocently holding hands.

* * *

The Continental Palace Hotel in Saigon still looked pretty much as it had done in Joseph Mankiewicz's 1958 film adaptation of Graham Greene's novel, *The Quiet American*, though the pavement *terrasse* had been removed as it offered too easy a target for suicide bombers. The hotel was the place most foreign journalists gathered when not at press briefings. Young Vietnamese boys offering to shine one's shoes or selling copies of the Stars and Stripes newspaper buzzed around like flies. Most of the Western journos looked bored as they sipped their drinks and waited for a story to happen, but I had made up my mind even before I arrived in Vietnam not to mingle with them. This was not just because I feared that seasoned war correspondents might take exception to an upstart newcomer with no appropriate qualifications who had just celebrated his 19th birthday but also because I had decided not to write about the War from a war correspondent's point of view, in terms of battles, advances and retreats, but rather to look at how the War was affecting the lives and livelihoods of ordinary Vietnamese, especially in the villages – more the approach of a human geographer or even a sociologist. This would result in a series of feature articles, rather than news stories; I imagined, correctly, that these would be more appealing to the Manchester Evening News, the Geographical Magazine and other outlets in the UK.

138

That meant that I would need to have good contacts within the Vietnamese Ministry of Agriculture in particular. Michael Counsell was especially helpful in opening doors at the British, American and German Embassies, where I got the necessary introductions. Meanwhile, I had managed to meet up with Cham's elder sister and her brother, who were both based in Saigon. They were eager to tell me about the life of young people such as themselves. Cham was still at the family home in Nhatrang, having failed to get transport down to Saigon, but her sister had apparently been at the airport to meet me the day I arrived, though somehow we had failed to link up.

On the first Sunday in Saigon, Michael Counsell suggested diffidently that if I wished to accompany him to morning service at his church I would be welcome, or if I preferred, both the Quakers and the Baha'i had bases within easy walking distance from his villa. As I had lost all interest in the established Church of England and felt alienated from its repetitive rituals, fate seemed to have offered me the opportunity to attend my first Quaker Meeting. This took place in the living room of a Scottish paediatrician, Dr Macaulay, and his socialist, Quaker wife. She hailed from Sale in Cheshire, on the outskirts of Manchester, and quite understood why I had fled my home territory. The Saigon Friends Meeting for Worship was a very small but clearly well-integrated group of Quakers and Attenders, including an occupational therapist and peace campaigner from London called Peggie Preston, a Japanese aid worker, Masako Yamanouchi, and a couple of young Americans. One of the latter, Clark, had just arrived in Saigon to be the link person for the American Friends Service Committee (AFSC), which was doing under-the-radar shuttle diplomacy and reconciliation work between North and South Vietnam, as well as being active in the anti-War movement in the United States. When Clark moved into his house in Saigon, the first thing he did was to dismantle the 12-foot high barbed wire fencing around it, which prompted his neighbours to immediately erect their own. Disconcertingly, someone had then painted graffiti in Vietnamese on his wall, saying, 'This house belongs to an American.'

* * *

Although I have considered myself semi-Quaker for about four years, having sometimes called in at the Friends Meeting House in Mount Street, Manchester, to collect literature about the Society of Friends on my way home from school, this was the first time for me to attend a Friends' Meeting. I found the silence very restful and it is wonderful to be put in a compulsory meditating position. I find my mind not dwelling on the past or even analysing the present but instead contemplating the future. I am determined to do something worthwhile with my life, and in many ways I wish I could stay here in Vietnam, as there is clearly so much that could be done. Perhaps when I get to Cambodia I can apply for a visa to go to North Vietnam, though I know it is unlikely to be granted. Yet some of the Quakers working for the American Friends Service Committee have managed to go there to deliver humanitarian aid and there is even a British Consul-General in Hanoi.

* * *

Of all the people at the Friends Meeting in Saigon the one who would remain a dear friend until her death in London in 2007 was Peggie Preston. The daughter of a British tea planter, she was born in Assam in India in 1923 and served with distinction as a Bomber Command radio operator in the WAAF during the Second World War, before the futility of killing and the destruction of Dresden drove her to pacifism and the Quakers. After qualifying as a therapist she was based at the Baragwanath Hospital in Soweto, South Africa, for several years before moving to Vietnam. In Saigon she helped street children and the families of political prisoners, as well as her young patients at a paediatric clinic at Phu My, a large multi-purpose health institution run by Catholic nuns. There were about 1,500 people of all ages housed at Phu My, segregated by age or gender and medical condition. When I visited the children's polio ward with Peggie the tiny children screamed with pleasure and dragged themselves across the floor to cling to our legs, begging to be played with or just to be hoisted in the air. In the crèche in another section there were about a hundred babies in cots as well as a number of older children who were helping the nuns look after them. An Australian woman working there had been organising adoptions of some of the infants abroad, until President Nguyen Van Thieu put a stop to it. The adult wards contained some severely deformed and wounded people; in the TB section, some of the patients made paper toys which were then sold in the market, to help raise funds for the institution. Oxfam had donated a piggery to Phu My, to help it generate some further income, but the nuns also raised modest funds from rents from an odd assortment of paying guests, including an old man from Czechoslovakia who had previously been a music teacher in the mountain resort of Dalat and a matronly French woman who was simply waiting to be repatriated.

Peggie Preston insisted on being paid only a local employee's salary and said she was trying to bring about reconciliation in the world through living by example. She worked closely with Vietnamese monks who were protesting against the Thieu government and the War, some of whom set fire to themselves in the street to draw attention to the inhumanity and pointlessness of the conflict. Peggie often looked exhausted and she lived in a permanent state of anxiety that the Vietnamese police would come to arrest her for her activism and then deport her.

As my own visa was only valid for two weeks, I had to go to the Immigration Department to arrange an extension, noting melodramatically in my diary that it had the reputation of being the most corrupt institution in the world. Although it would be another six years before the Communists succeeded in taking over South Vietnam, the Tet Offensive had unnerved the population and constant rumours fanned by fifth columnists made many people fear an imminent Viet Cong attack, which meant that thousands were trying to find a way to get out of the country. For this they needed an exit visa, which was extremely hard to get, unless one bribed the officials in the Immigration Department sufficiently. The government was determined to stop a mass exodus and during my first week in the country it banned an issue of the American magazine Newsweek which contained an article revealing that President Thieu's wife had bought a villa in Switzerland and had deposited their children safely in Rome. There was a crush of people

141

at the Immigration Department pleading with stony-faced officials for exit stamps on my first visit, and I felt guilty for receiving special treatment as a foreign journalist there to extend my stay. Thanks to bureaucratic procedures this did nonetheless necessitate several further visits and yet more photographs, one of which I had to remove from my youth hostelling card as I had run out of spares. At least I never felt obliged to pay a bribe.

Walking more than a few yards in Saigon in the summer monsoon was exhausting because of the humidity, which left one's shirt drenched with sweat. Fortunately taxis were extremely cheap, if one bargained hard, especially the motorised pedicabs, in which the passenger sat in a sort of garden chair in the front while the driver on the motorised bike behind weaved his way among the thousands of motorcycles that clogged the streets. Michael Counsell generously let me stay at the vicarage until I was ready to travel out of the city, and at the Rex Hotel there was a military canteen at which I could use one of my ID cards to get lunch for 60 US cents. I may have become a cub foreign correspondent but I was still travelling with the economising mind-set of a backpacker.

Every few days I went to the Central Post Office to check whether I had any mail. In those pre-email days, the only way of keeping in touch with anyone was by having letters sent to Poste Restante at wherever one expected to be. International phone calls were prohibitively expensive and I never made one during the whole of my time in Asia. Letters did get through usually, though in Saigon this involved queueing in a line of anxious locals who were waiting for news from relatives who had managed to leave the country. I always had to insist that the counter clerks check for mail for me under both 'F' and 'J' as letters were filed arbitrarily by family or Christian name. When sending letters out, one had to post them through a hole in the wall inside the Central Post Office. Michael Counsell told me that if you peeked through the hole, you could see a government censor sitting at a table on the other side. This fellow caught the letters as they came through the hole and steamed them open to verify that there was nothing incriminating inside. I was determined to check if this was true, but being even taller than Michael, I had to bend almost double to look through the opening as

142

I pushed a letter through; sure enough a young censor was sitting there on the other side and he gave me a nervous smile when I caught his eye.

* * *

My first sortie out of Saigon was to Can Tho in the Mekong Delta, where there had been a lot of heavy fighting recently; it therefore seemed a good choice for research into how the War was affecting village life. Getting there involved an early morning flight from the Air America terminal at Than Son Nhut; the man sitting next to me on the plane asked breezily if I also worked for the CIA and was taken aback when I said I was British. I was expecting to be met at Can Tho airport, but as no-one was waiting there, I hopped on a military shuttle bus to the regional HQ of CORDS (Civil Operations and Revolutionary Development Support), where I found a man called Rholfo whom I had met a few days before in Saigon. He seemed amazed that I had actually made it, as a party of six South Vietnamese dignitaries had been due to arrive that morning but they had cancelled because of reports of fighting in the area. A whole day's programme had been arranged for them and Mr Rholfo was concerned that the villagers along the route would be disappointed if no-one turned up, so the obvious solution was for me to take the dignitaries' place. I thought I would be a poor substitute, but in fact the reception everywhere was warm and I was viewed with great curiosity in my white shirt and linen slacks, Harold's Canon camera hung from a strap round my neck. The locals had probably never seen a young white man not in army uniform.

Accompanied by a guide-interpreter who had the same name as President Thieu, I was taken to visit the young man who had produced the highest yield of rice per hectare in the region with the aid of a new strain introduced from Taiwan. His elderly father received us, proffering a plate of raw fish, which Mr Thieu whispered to me I must eat, otherwise our host would be deeply offended; washed down with what tasted like fermented pear juice, it wasn't too bad. The old man told us that his four older sons were all in the South Vietnamese armed forces but one had been kidnapped

143

recently by the Viet Cong and he feared the youth would never be seen again. Because his family was so closely aligned with the Saigon government the youngest son could only farm within sight of the road as otherwise he might be captured by the VC as well. His father proudly showed me the trophies his son had won for his agricultural prowess: a hideous cigarette lighter fixed to the top of a plastic miniature Roman column and a shield from the Lions Club.

As I climbed into the white van that was driving us round, an artillery gun nearby suddenly let off a deafening volley, making me jump. Mr Thieu shrugged in embarrassment as he explained that the Viet Cong were not far away, but I should not worry as they usually stayed down in tunnels during the day, emerging at night to collect rice and taxes from the peasantry. This would become the peg for one of my features for the Manchester Evening News, which was headlined 'Where the village tax man calls after dark'.

The next stop was a village so calm and picture-perfect that it seemed a million miles from the War. The main road ran between a river on one side and a drainage ditch on the other, and there were about a dozen bamboo houses dotted among the palm trees and other vegetation, out of which poured a horde of little children, yelling with excitement at our arrival. Over the other side of the little river were some paddy fields, which were the object of our visit, but I was horrified to see that the 'bridge' one would have to cross to get there consisted merely of a series of narrow tree trunks resting on forked branches about six feet above the water, the only handrail being a row of bamboo poles. The village children were by now running back and forth across this structure, laughing, sensing my alarm at the prospect of falling off it into the water. Mr Thieu took off his shoes and nimbly demonstrated how to cross without losing one's balance, but I had frozen in panic. Using the lame excuse that I was worried that my camera might fall into the river, I waited until one of the villagers bought a small boat alongside, to ferry me across. The children stood in a row on the 'bridge', howling with laughter.

Suddenly I am back at school, in the gym, standing paralysed at the bottom of the wall-bars. The gym master is there getting red in the face as he shouts at me not to be such a nelly and to get up there pronto, while all around the other boys are jeering. My hands are on

144

the bars but my feet are stuck to the floor as if set in concrete. I shut
my eyes and want to disappear but I can't block out the sound of the
mocking laughter. I think I am going to pass out.

'Are you alright?' Mr Thieu asked as he gently took hold of my
arm. I opened my eyes and let him lead me to the little boat. 'Yes,
fine, thank you. Just a little tired. It was an early start.'

* * *

Can Tho was considered to be a 'secure' town where foreigners
could walk around during daylight in comparative safety, but it was a
miserable place, consisting mainly of a crossroads and uninspiring
one- and two-storey concrete buildings. Thanks to the monsoon the
streets were covered in thick black sludge that splashed up as a
constant stream of military vehicles went by. Many of the lorries had
shattered windscreens or neat little bullet-holes where Viet Cong
sympathisers had taken a pot shot at them. Next to the dreary little
functional hotel where I stayed on Ben Xe Moi was Olga's
restaurant, where they served plates of tempura shrimp and rice to
staff from USAID and other American personnel, who flirted with
the Vietnamese waitress. It reminded me of some of the places I had
seen on Okinawa, part of an economy that thrived only because of
the large US military presence that was itself nonetheless a source of
barely concealed resentment. The Americans in Can Tho were very
security-conscious because of Viet Cong activity and some of the
bars that catered to the GIs were completed enclosed in barbed wire
netting cages. At night, the soldiers would return to the safety of a
large military air-base.

I visited this army camp, which had been made to resemble small
town America as far as possible, with a PX store selling discounted
popular brands and a canteen that served hot dogs and chilli con
carne and offered more flavours of ice-cream than I had ever seen.
The young soldiers, teenagers like me, joked and smoked but when I
interviewed some of them their underlying nervousness soon came to
the surface. 'The trouble with these damned gooks is you never know
which of them is a Commie,' one lad from Texas told me. 'You're
out on patrol and there they are in their black pyjamas by the side of

145

the road just standing staring at you and you just know they want to stick a knife right through you. But we have to pussy-foot around them. But, shit, the Koreans know how to deal with them. Man, those Koreans are tough! They don't stand for no nonsense from them gooks, no Sir!'

The South Korean forces in Vietnam did indeed have a fearsome reputation. Over a period of nearly ten years from 1964, the military dictator in Seoul, Park Chung-Hee, sent about 300,000 Koreans to fight in Vietnam and their hatred of the Communists was visceral, the memories of the devastating Korean War still part of their collective consciousness. They were notorious for the brutality of their interrogation of suspected Viet Cong and in February 1968 they had been responsible for a massacre of several dozen Vietnamese civilians at Phong Ni and Phong Nhat. Of course, the American killings at My Lai the following month were even worse, though full details had not yet leaked out while I was in Vietnam. My minder in Can To, Mr Thieu, was philosophical about the collateral damage of civilian deaths in the confusion of the War, pointing out that virtually every family had been affected in one way or another. When he invited me to visit his home at Bien Thuy I discovered that the modest dwelling housed not only him, his wife and their four children but also his brother, his wife and their six children. His brother's house had been occupied by the Viet Cong during the Tet Offensive so the Americans had bombed it to smithereens. At least the family had escaped intact.

* * *

As my penfriend Cham was still finding it impossible to find transport down to Saigon, once I had successfully got my visa extended I managed to get on a military flight to go to visit her in Nhatrang. The aircraft was a Lockheed C130 Hercules in which I sat surrounded by both American and Vietnamese troops. Frustratingly one could not see anything of the countryside over which we were flying, though I knew a lot of it would be pockmarked with bomb craters or scarred by chemical defoliants. From the airbase at Nhatrang I hitch-hiked into town then I walked to Cham's family

146

home, which was part of a shopping block on the main street, Doc Lap. Most of the ground floor was empty, apart from a small kitchen and an adjacent dining-area. Cham's parents were at home when I got there; her father looked much older than his 60 years. He greeted me formally while his wife, who was clearly unwell, brought us cups of tea. We then sat in silence waiting for Cham to come home.

As it had been Cham's letter back in January that had been the spark that lit the flame that drove me to embark on this project of coming to Vietnam there was an inevitable degree of nervous anticipation on both sides, but when she arrived, demure in her pastel-coloured *ao dai*, smiling but painfully shy, neither of us knew what to say to each other. I had the awkward feeling that I was there under false pretences. From her point of view, I had come to Vietnam specifically to see her, whereas for me now she was incidental. It was the War and the wider canvas of Asia that were important. I was no longer the schoolboy I had been even six months before, eager for new adventures but still largely naïve and experiencing Asia vicariously through letters from my penfriends. I was no longer a passive spectator of world events but was experiencing some of them at first hand, even writing about them, and I was sure that this would be the sort of life on the road that I would want to lead in future, not a comfortable existence with a steady job, a wife and two kids back in Europe, which I knew was the sort of idyll Cham had in mind. Besides, when I looked at Cham, with whom I had discussed so much in letters, I knew we could only be friends, nothing more. I was not ready for any sort of intimate relationship with anyone, of either sex.

I had enjoyed meeting Cham's siblings in Saigon, with whom conversations had mainly been about their college life and local culture. But her eldest brother, whom I now encountered in Nhatrang, was a very different character, full of resentment against the Americans. He railed against the effect that GIs had on towns like Nhatrang and deplored the fact that local people were obliged to eat imported American rice, which he said was a disgrace for a rice-producing country like Vietnam. He was not a very comfortable person to be with but I admired his frankness and his insights were informative. Listening to him I also realised that my presence in the

147

household was deeply compromising for the family. They had put the message out that I was not American, but British, but the fact that I was staying there – in the best bedroom in the house, sleeping under a bright blue mosquito net – would inevitably fuel gossip about my relationship with Cham. Her father tactfully requested that the two of us should never be seen outside together, just the two of us, or else her reputation would be ruined. Instead, we should go about with a group of her friends, both boys and girls, which is exactly what we did over the coming days.

Nhatrang had the reputation of being the safest town in South Vietnam; certainly there was less barbed wire and fewer military posts than in the other places I had visited. Situated on the coast, with fine sandy beaches, it still retained a little of the charm of a French colonial seaside resort, though its narrow, tree-lined roads, including Doc Lap, were pot-holed and full of rubbish. Along the shore there were some beautiful villas and from the celebrated Hon Chong rocks outside town there were fine views out towards several islands. Our little group of friends travelled everywhere on Hondas, with me sat behind one of the boys whose waist was so slim that my hands almost reached right round it. Not surprisingly, we got some odd looks from people we passed on the road.

One afternoon we rode out to the eighth century Po Nagar Cham Hindu temple, whose central image is a statue of the goddess Yan Po Nagar, sitting cross-legged. Several of the statues in the small complex were dressed in colourful clothes. Cham's girlfriends soon had me kneeling in one chapel, incense sticks burning in my hands, while a woman banged a gong at the altar. I then had to draw a numbered rod from a pot; I plucked number 48, which I was assured was quite auspicious. A fortune-teller then declared that my short-term future was bright, but that I would fail an exam the following year, which did not particularly bother me, considering how many I had failed at school. The heavens opened on our way back into town, which left Doc Lap three inches deep in water.

The sky had cleared when the gang of Cham's friends arrived at the house at seven the following morning to go to the beach, which was how they liked to spend their Sundays. At the port we boarded a flat-bottomed landing craft like the ones the Japanese used in the

148

Second World War and we chugged over to a fishing village on one of the offshore islands. The fishermen lived in bamboo huts among the coconut palms and hordes of children and ducks scurried around. We found a secluded spot on the beach where the girls laid out a picnic lunch and the boys set up a portable gramophone, to play songs by Adamo and Sylvie. It was surreal hearing these French popular songs against the backdrop of the War, and I suspected that for my young companions listening to them was a form of escapism. 'If you look over to those hills over there,' one boy nonetheless said, pointing towards the mainland, 'you can sometimes spot the Viet Cong moving around.' But being short-sighted I would not have been able to see them, even if they had been there.

* * *

The cool air of the mountains, when I left Nhatrang for Dalat, was a welcome relief. The hill-town's airport was little more than a strip of red laterite with a small hut at one side in which sat a rather dozy African-American from the deep South who nonetheless finally managed to get through to the local CORDS office by telephone and arrange for me to be picked up. I was installed in the misleadingly named Modern Hotel in the centre of town, right opposite a two-storey market that had vegetable and flower stalls on the ground floor and clothes upstairs, including piles of hand-knitted woollies for children. The Modern was an establishment famed throughout Vietnam for its hot and cold running women, but as a notice on its wall proclaimed it had just been declared off-limits to 'Free World Personnel' following a fracas involving a GI. The young Vietnamese women who were sitting around in the lobby obviously hoped that at least some men would nonetheless still patronise the establishment. The lady in charge decided that I looked so young and innocent that she dubbed me Baby San and called me that for the whole of my stay. She and her husband had four sweet little children with a fifth on the way, which gave the place an incongruous homely atmosphere.

The French had used the town as a cool summer retreat, rather like the British hill stations in India, and there were several churches in the town, now mainly catering to the Vietnamese population, among whom were many Montagnards, the indigenous Degar people of the central highlands. Most of the Degar were fervently anti-Communist and their hatred of the Viet Cong was sealed when the VC massacred over 250 of their number at the village of Dak Son in 1967. The American Special Forces trained some of the Montagnard men in so-called unconventional warfare to stop Viet Cong infiltration and to disrupt the Ho Chi Minh Trail, the cross country supply line from North Vietnam to the South that ran through the neighbouring countries of Laos and Cambodia. Physically distinct from the more pale skinned and often willowy ethnic Vietnamese, the Degar men did indeed look tough, and it was probably partly because of their presence that Dalat was considered to be a relatively safe town. In Dalat the nightly curfew began at the unusually late hour of 10pm; on the first night I was caught unprepared, as the siren itself was located right near the hotel. It sounded just like an air raid alert, so when it went off I thought we about to come under attack. The following evening, as I was preparing for bed, there was a knock on my door; this turned out to be US military police who were checking the hotel for any servicemen who were ignoring the ban. They were astonished to find a young European there instead.

A little way outside Dalat there was a village housing refugees from North Vietnam who were cultivating vegetables on neat terraces on the surrounding hillsides. Before going to Vietnam I had always pictured it in the black-and-white tones of war photographs and television newsreels but here I was struck more than ever by how green everything was. The villagers in their conical hats were picturesque against this verdant backdrop, but often when they saw a camera pointing in their direction they ran away. A man from CORDS explained that some of the older people were superstitious that their spirit might be captured by the camera, never to return. Yet children always gathered excitedly around asking to be photographed, even though in those pre-digital camera days there was no way of showing them their picture.

* * *

Walking by the side of the lake at Dalat reminds me strongly of Windermere in England's Lake District, though some of the more substantial houses with their steep sloping rooves looked positively Alpine. But as soon as I thought of Windermere I stopped short, searching back into my memory. The school trip to the Lake District in my first year at MGS didn't go there, so why can I now see Windermere so clearly in my mind? Then I remembered that I did go there once, perhaps later that same year; certainly not much after that. Harold had decided it would be good for me to learn to fish trout, even though I had not the slighted desire, so he drove me up to Scotland via the Lake District. We stayed in a small guesthouse in Tomintoul in what was then Banffshire and which claimed to be the highest village in the Scottish Highlands. We only went fishing once; I remember standing in waders borrowed from the hotel, several feet out into the river. Harold had bought fishing rods that had to be slotted together and a box of flies, handmade, multi-coloured and rather beautiful. These we cast into the shallow river in the hope of snaring trout, but nothing bit and after a while Harold became impatient and accused me of scaring the fish away by splashing about too much in the water. It was true that I was restless and actually I was hoping we wouldn't catch any fish, as I could not bear the thought of ripping the hook from their mouths. That night Harold came into my room and then... I can't remember what happened. Maybe I don't want to remember. Was Rosemary with us on this trip? I don't think so, but I can't remember. I try hard but there is nothing there in the recesses of my memory. It's like a great heavy curtain has fallen down, preventing me accessing that part of my past. But even trying to think about it makes me start to feel anxious and beads of sweat come out on my forehead.

What I do remember is that afterwards, having abandoned Tomintoul and any pretence at fishing, Harold moved us to the grand Turnberry Hotel in Ayrshire, so he could play golf. It was an enormously long white building – more like a terrace of smart houses – and there I was left to my own devices. Whatever happened in Tomintoul had sated his interest in me for a while, and all he wanted was for me to scram.

The journey back to Saigon was made in a series of hops, from Dalat to Kamh Ranh Bay, then on to Nhatrang before I finally found a place on a flight to the capital. From the windows of the Air America plane out of Kamh Ranh Bay I was able to watch US bombers attacking a Viet Cong emplacement in the hills near Nhatrang, the impact visible but inaudible over the whirring engines of our own craft. How many civilian casualties there might be in this operation was anyone's guess, and they could be dismissed by the US military as collateral damage. This was long before the age of video games, yet for many on that Air America flight what was happening was like playing a game: a war game, in which the only aim was to win, at whatever cost.

From Nhatrang I was put on a 7-seater propeller plane that had to fly low, giving me a grandstand view of the bomb craters and areas of defoliated forest down below. The pilot pointed out the most dramatic war damage with pride. I was reminded of the black-and-white wartime American movies of action against the Japanese, shown on afternoon television back in England, in which clean-cut All American heroes battle for the survival of liberty in the face of the Yellow Peril; 25 years on it was if nothing had changed. The Vietnamese were dehumanised in the eyes of so many Americans in Vietnam and dehumanisation is one of the stages in a progression that can eventually lead to genocide.

As Michael Counsell had another house-guest staying at the vicarage when I returned to Saigon, I was taken in by the Macaulays. At their house I read a long and brilliant article by an American journalist in a back issue of the New Yorker describing the situation in Quang Ngai province; details were just beginning to leak out of massacres of civilians by US troops there.

It certainly is enough to turn anybody against the American presence here. Many of the kinds of incident he cited and the people he mentioned I myself have come across and I find myself agreeing with him entirely. At last my position on Vietnam is completely clear in my own mind and it is different from that of even a few days ago. I now can find no justification for the American presence in view of the methods they are using and the way that they are corrupting the moral and cultural aspects of Vietnamese society. I am thus in favour of a complete withdrawal of foreign manpower.

* * *

Given my newly developed distaste for the War, being in Vietnam was no longer so much of an enjoyable adventure, in which I could just jump on a plane and be taken everywhere and shown everything. I felt I had seen enough. I began to understand why some of the embittered old war correspondents in the bar at the Continental Palace Hotel had turned to drink. It was time to move on. I sympathised with the young GI I met at Thon San Nhut airport who was on his way home and who said, 'I've been here 15 months. Never been shot at, never shot anyone. I've had the good part of the War.' He was lucky, as thousands of others had seen and done things that would mark them for the rest of their lives, making it impossible for them to reintegrate into their small town communities back home. As I noted in my diary, although my time in Vietnam had made me a pacifist it had also shown me that physically I was afraid of nothing. Most of all, I did not fear death. Indeed, at times in the weeks to come I felt I would welcome it.

* * *

From the window of the Air Vietnam flight from Saigon to Phnom Penh the bomb craters on the Cambodian side of the frontier were glaringly visible. So much for the American claims that they were not violating Cambodian territory in their War to contain Communism. From the air, the Cambodian landscape was very similar to Vietnam's, but as the plane descended to the runway it was clear that the architecture of the buildings was strikingly different. As I would quickly discover, there was a marked cultural shift as well, which partly explained why Cambodians and Vietnamese regarded each other somewhat warily. I had suspected as much from the letters I had received over the preceding couple of years from my ethnic Chinese Cambodian penfriend, Chan-Hong. As with Cham in

Vietnam, I had linked up with him through Les Amis du Courier, and although he was nowhere near as prolific a letter writer as Cham, he had told me enough to prepare me for a different experience. That contrast was accentuated by the fact that Chan-Hong came from a very different sort of family. He was at Phnom Penh airport to meet me, along with a couple of friends and his family's chauffeur, who drove us back to the villa where the 17-year-old Chan-Hong was living with 11 brothers and sisters and several servants. His parents were away on an extended visit to France. The French influence was much more marked in Phnom Penh than it had been in Saigon and on my first evening there Chan-Hong and his mates took me to a cinema to see Raoul André's entertaining thriller *Les Femmes D'Abord* starring Eddie Constantine.

My mind was nonetheless still preoccupied with the war in Vietnam. That very first day in Phnom Penh I went on my own to the North Vietnamese Embassy to sound out the possibility of going to Hanoi. I was surprised to find that unlike the other Communist embassies in town it had no glass-fronted board of propaganda photographs outside and when I was ushered in to a tastefully decorated sitting room and given a cup of tea the only sign identifying the place for what it was, was a single black-and-white photograph of Ho Chi Minh. The Ambassador was unavailable but the young diplomat who saw me gave me an application form to complete, though he warned me that it was unlikely that permission to visit would come through before the following year given the war conditions. At least I had made the effort.

Like Cham in Nhatrang, Chan-Hong tended to move round with a tight group of friends, which in his case involved three brothers, Tong, Sung and Kim, the last of these being just 16 years old but a keen judo practitioner, constantly showing off his strength. I was struck by how tactile the boys were, forever touching each other, joshing or simply having their arms round each other. They happily went through the meagre contents of my little suitcase without any inhibition or embarrassment, but were shocked when they saw a picture postcard, wondering how anyone could write a personal message on a card which could be read by any stranger before it reached its destination. Phnom Penh itself was nonetheless definitely

154

worthy of picture postcards, with its ornate temples and palaces. Chan-Hong took me to one of the latter to see Prince Norodom Sihanouk's private museum, which displayed all the presents he had received from dignitaries around the world as well as numerous letters of commendation. Sihanouk had been King from 1941 to 1955 (and would be again from 1993 to 2004) and there was a personality cult around him almost as pervasive as that around Mao Zedong in China. Sihanouk's name was associated with practically every national enterprise, no matter how small.

* * *

Early one morning, Chan-Hong, the three brothers and I went to the main market in Phnom Penh to catch a bus to Siem Riap, a 320-km journey that would take over eight hours. The bus was an ancient American Dodge that had seats that stretched across the width of the vehicle, with a door on one end of the row, so five people could sit together. It looked as if it had been designed to transport schoolchildren in the American Mid-West. That was no problem for my young companions but painfully awkward for me, being 6'2" tall. On the roof of the bus was piled all the passengers' luggage as well as building materials, several bicycles and a motorcycle. As soon as we had left the city and crossed the Mekong River by way of a small ferry the contrast between the rural areas and Phnom Penh was evident. Typical *pailotte* grass huts along the road were built on stilts with an open doorway at both the front and back, and a ladder running down from the rear doorway. Interspersed with these huts were a number of more robust wooden dwellings, a few of which had corrugated iron rooves. The bus stopped not just at all the major villages but also on request, passengers indicating when they wanted to get off to a scruffy little conductor who used a whistle to let the driver know. Every so often the bus would stop in front of a house and someone on the roof would throw some articles from up there down onto the verge below. The villagers clearly had a simple life but no-one looked malnourished. Unlike the Cambodians of Chinese or Vietnamese origin, the Khmers were quite dark-skinned, sturdy and muscular.

155

Arriving in Siem Reap in the late afternoon we found a cheap hotel and booked into a room with two beds; Tong Hay and I would share one while the other three boys squeezed into the other. They were quite used to sleeping together and in fact disliked sleeping alone. On those occasions when sleeping alone was unavoidable, Chan-Hong explained, they liked to hold a cylindrical bolster as a comforter between their legs. Wandering round the town in the evening we came across a black and yellow snake by the roadside which the boys recognised as highly venomous. Some local men, standing at a safe distance, started attacking it with broomsticks and succeeded in stunning it, so it could be pushed onto the road where it would be run over and killed.

The following morning we were up at 6.30 to hire a *remorque*, a sort of trailer powered by a motorbike, to travel out to Angkor Wat. In peacetime this area would be full of tourists, but with the Vietnam War spilling over into Cambodia and the summer monsoon in full spate we were alone as we puttered along under the shade of tall trees. Angkor Wat itself was so much bigger and more majestic than I had imagined, half swallowed by the forest, with just a few Buddhist monks in their saffron or orange robes moving about the structure, stopping briefly to gaze at our little band. The great gates in the outer wall of the main compound were guarded by two lines of stone warriors holding a vast serpent. Several of the temples at Bayon nearby were almost completely submerged under the vegetation; some of the gates and spires were caged in the roots of colossal trees. In some places restoration was obviously taking place, though no archaeologists were visible. At one stage we did spot a couple of German visitors and in a clearing we came across a large group of Cambodians sitting on the ground having a picnic, chatting and playing music. Altogether we were at the site for nearly eight hours. Tong and I wandered off to explore some of the more remote monuments when the others had tired. There were all sorts of bird and animal noises coming from the forest around us and we kept a sharp eye out for snakes, though the only one we saw at Angkor was a bright blue specimen that dropped down from a tree right by the side of the *remorque* where the others were stood waiting for us.

Back in Siem Reap in the evening, the others had oeufs couvrés *for supper – fertilised eggs which are eaten about two days before they hatch. Absolutely revolting and enough to persuade one to become vegetarian, which I always think Buddhists ought to be anyway. Oddly enough, the eggs set me thinking on the subject of abortion, and I have come to the conclusion that there is no moral justification for abortion unless the life of the mother is in severe danger, or the baby will be completely deformed. No-one has the right to deprive a half-live entity of life. I wonder if my mother would have aborted me if she had had the option, but I suspect not. I can only be grateful to her for letting me live, even if the adoption was not a success. So I find myself totally disagreeing with David Steel, though I understand the motivation for his Abortion Act. In this kind of way this trip is giving me the opportunity for considerable meditation and reflection, so that I am beginning to be more sure of my own feelings and beliefs.*

* * *

We returned to Phnom Penh via Cambodia's second city Battambang, which meant travelling right round the huge lake of Tonle Sap. The sizeable market in Battambang was full of goods from Thailand and there was evidently a good deal of smuggling going on across the Thai-Cambodia border. That may be why several of the hotels we tried to check into refused to accept me as the proprietors suspected I was a journalist. Having asserted my status as a young foreign correspondent in Vietnam I now had to revert to playing the role of a student traveller, in order to deflect suspicion. The one hotel that did not turn us away was clearly a brothel, but as with so many of its kind in Indo-China, it was friendly and welcoming without insisting that one become a client of one of the girls waiting downstairs.

Back in Phnom Penh I headed for the Embassy of the Provisional Revolutionary Government of South Vietnam (PRGSV), which called itself 'neutral' but in fact represented the Communist forces that were due to take over in Saigon if or when the Americans withdrew and the current government collapsed, as I was pretty sure one day it would. The Second Secretary there explained that there was no government HQ as such in South Vietnam, though oddly there was a Cuban Embassy to the Revolutionary Government of South Vietnam, hidden somewhere in the jungle. He said the PRGSV opposed the notion of internationally-monitored elections, which were part of a possible peace settlement being promoted in the West; instead they argued that any democratic exercise should be an entirely Vietnamese affair. When I asked him why it was necessary for the Viet Cong to carry out terrorist attacks, such as the bomb that had gone off in the Central Post Office while I had been in Saigon, he was unable to provide a satisfactory answer.

The next expedition with Chan-Hong and the boys was to the coast at Kep, a fashionable resort (at least in season) where Chan-Hong's family had a small vacation home near the beach. Getting there involved a four-hour journey to Kampot on a train donated by Australia through the Colombo Plan. The floor of the carriage was made of wooden planks and one could see the tracks through the gaps in between them. At the station in Kampot there was an exhibition of photographs showing Cambodians rounding up Viet Cong. From there we took a *remorque* to Kep. The little house reminded me of the cottage Harold and Rosemary used to rent during August at Porthdinllaen (and where coincidentally they would now soon be heading), fairly basic but fit for purpose. Chan-Hong, Seng and Kim all had camp beds to sleep on, while Tong and Yan (an even younger boy always referred to by the others as 'Le Petit') and I lay down together on the floor under a giant mosquito net. Unfortunately the weather was dreadful, so apart from a couple of very quick swims and an occasional walk round the village, we were forced to sit indoors most of the time, playing cards or the Chinese board game Go as the rain thundered down on the roof. It was so cold that the three boys on the camp beds pushed them all together so they could huddle together to try to generate some warmth.

Back in Phnom Penh we found Chan-Hong's family household in pandemonium, as a telegram had been delivered announcing that his father and mother were going to arrive back from France the following day. All the boys appeared to be frightened of the father and Chan-Hong begged me to leave before his parents arrived; I guess I must have been sleeping in their bed. I had not planned on departing Cambodia quite so soon, but fortunately a next door neighbour, Mr Nguyen, an affluent Vietnamese, kindly offered to put me up. Yet when Chan-Hong came round to Mr Nguyen's house the following day to take me to meet his father he proved to be a genial fellow, unexpectedly youthful looking, though his wife was quite haggard, perhaps from having borne 12 children over a short span of years. It transpired that Chan-Hong's father hoped to send him to England to study if he managed to get through his Baccalauréat. Mr Nguyen had the same aspiration for his daughter, so I found myself being despatched to the British Council offices the next day to get them some information on suitable courses. I never discovered whether either of them succeeded in going to England as I soon lost touch with Chan-Hong, unlike with Cham in Vietnam. When the time came for me to leave Cambodia for Bangkok, Chan-Hong and a couple of his friends went with me to the airport to see me off. I can only hope his family did manage to escape to Europe before the fanatical Khmer Rouge took over Cambodia in 1975 as otherwise they would certainly have been exterminated.

* * *

Bangkok was the only place on the whole of the Asia trip where I had a familiar face to greet me: Rosemary's nephew (and Harold's godson) Jeremy Bishop, who was working at the Ford Foundation office in the Thai capital. He lived in a smart apartment in a modern block off the Sukhumvit Road, whose landlady was a minor Thai royal. As Jeremy was a singularly generous person anyway and was busy enjoying the life of a still relatively young bachelor expat on a good salary, he had a busy social life that led him to many of the best restaurants and club facilities on offer. On the very first evening, he took me to dinner at the President Hotel's coffee shop, before heading on to the British Club, where he played a game of squash. I seized the opportunity to weigh myself, registering 74.5kg, which confirmed my impression that I had lost all my puppy fat.

The first few days in Bangkok were largely spent organising my ongoing travel, which required a whole new batch of visas and permits. Jeremy's servant had washed and ironed my one white short-sleeved shirt and the fawn linen trousers so I looked presentable and I had 40 copies of a new passport photo made, many of which were soon stuck on application forms filled out manually in duplicate or even triplicate at various embassies. At the British Embassy I obtained the letter of recommendation testifying to my good character that was necessary in order to get a visa for Laos; the fact that I was able to put Jeremy's smart address as my current abode doubtless helped expedite matters. While waiting for that to be processed I asked one of the Ford Foundation's drivers, a young Muslim confusingly called Him, to take me to the Nepalese Embassy to begin the application process there. Him had no idea that Nepal existed, let alone its embassy, so we stopped at the Indian Embassy to ask for directions. When we later arrived at the building indicated, I was cordially greeted by a lady in a sari, who laughed and said British subjects did not need visas. She then handed me a collection of travel brochures and wished me a good stay in her country; when I looked at them I saw that they were all about Sri Lanka. Outside I found that Him had also discovered he had brought me to the wrong place and he sheepishly drove me round to the Nepalese nearby. It turned out it had only been open a few days, so Him could be forgiven for not knowing it. Next, it was the turn of the Burmese Embassy, where an official confirmed what I had heard from other travellers I had met along the way in South East Asia that although tourist visas to his country were rarely given, I could get a 24-hour transit visa if I bought an air ticket from Bangkok to Calcutta on Union of Burma Airways, as that route required a change of planes and an overnight stay in Rangoon, which was a city I was particularly keen to see because of George Orwell's writings. In the 1920s Orwell had worked in Burma as an employee of the Indian Imperial Police, an experience that helped shape his attitude to oppression and injustice in all its forms.

My mind numbed from all the hours of diplomatic bureaucracy, I asked Jeremy one evening to take me to see some of Bangkok's seedier night-life along Phetburi Extension, a new road along which a string of girlie bars had sprung up. Bangkok had developed a niche role for itself as the preferred location for Rest and Recuperation –

R&R – for American soldiers on short term leave from the Vietnam War. As a predominantly Buddhist country, Thailand had a relatively relaxed attitude to sexual desire and entertainment of all kinds and the government obviously thought it was in the country's interest economically and politically to allow appropriate facilities to operate for their American allies. The Thai girlie bars were far raunchier than their Vietnamese or Okinawan equivalents. It was still quite early when we got to the Green Dragon, where one of the gogo girls was flashing her knickers at a group of braying GIs; another had a fluorescent butterfly stuck to her bare midriff. There were several other customers who were clearly just sightseeing like us. Because Jeremy was extremely tall, he towered over the locals, prompting one giggling girl who was seated on a barstool to reach up and tweek his nose. Many of the girls who worked in the bars along Phetburi Extension or at more up-market establishments elsewhere in the city, such as C'est Si Bon and the Mona Lisa, came from impoverished villages in the north of Thailand and they sent most of the money they earned back home to feed their families. Some of the girls would pester clients for coins for the juke box or would wheedle to be bought a drink, but in the 'heavier' establishments the working girls sat on the other side of a two-way mirror, each of them wearing a number so men could choose which girl they wanted as a dance partner or as a companion for the night.

There were also many massage parlours in Bangkok, where for US$3 one could have an hour's massage, any further service being subject to a generous tip. A friend of Jeremy's insisted that he take me to one of his favourite places where there were over 100 girls and women on view. I chose one who spoke English and who must have been nearly twice my age. She led me down a long carpeted corridor to a room where she removed her white linen coat, similar to a doctor's gown, as soon as she had closed the door, to reveal a bathing costume underneath. She told me to strip and get into a sunken bath where she soaped me down, including my private parts; then she sat me down on a chair while she gave me a pedicure. Finally, I was directed to a couch for the massage. My expectation of a nice, soothing experience was soon dispelled as she pulled, bent and kicked various muscles painfully. No doubt some men would

161

have derived erotic pleasure from this treatment but I could not wait for it to stop. However, I was even more startled and unprepared when she suddenly removed her hands and threw herself on the couch, declaring, 'That's enough massage!' I did not feel in the slightest bit sexually excited, only highly embarrassed, and I was peeved that Jeremy's friend had not warned me that this was going to happen. I made my excuses, as the masseuse laughed merrily at my innocence. Once I was dressed and safely out of the building I found Jeremy's friend leaning against the wall of the establishment, a big grin on his face.

* * *

Jeremy took me for a weekend to the beach resort of Pattaya, which was nowhere near as sleazy in 1969 as parts of it are now, or at least not the part where we stayed in a bungalow that belonged to one of Jeremy's Thai friends. Jeremy complained that the facilities were not up to his usual standards but to me they seemed quite luxurious after the place I had stayed in at Kep in Cambodia with Chan-Hong and his friends. I tried water-skiing for the first time – having avoided doing so in Porthdinllaen in Wales, as I was sure I would fall over and be jeered at – and to my surprise found that I took to it easily. The bay at Pattaya, with its clear blue water and the green hills behind, looked magnificent and the weather was kind. We ate in a great seafood restaurant in the evening and I was sad to leave, but Jeremy had to be back for work on the Monday morning and I had planned to catch a 7am bus that day from Bangkok to Nong Kai, 655kms away.

* * *

The bus to Nong Kai was a modern coach and the road was well-paved. Unlike its Cambodian counterparts, the bus did not stop every few minutes, which meant that it only took 10-and-a-half hours to reach its destination, having previously dropped off most of its passengers at the town of Udorn, where there was a large American military base. I hurried to the bank of the Mekong River so I would

162

be there before the Thai immigration post closed and I was able to pass speedily through to the landing stage. There, a small motor-boat was moored waiting to take passengers over the Mekong to Laos for a fare of five Thai baht or 10 US cents. That was the only legal way into the country other than flying to the capital Vientiane.

On the Laotian side of the river there was no proper docking place; instead one had to manoeuvre oneself dextrously along a plank to get to the shore without falling in and then climb a series of slippery, muddy steps to the top of the river bank. I was glad the only luggage I had brought with me was my small YMCA shoulder bag. From the Laotian immigration post I got a taxi into Vientiane, accepting the driver's suggestion that I check into the Hotel Constellation in the rue Samsentai. Though quite small, this hotel was something of a Vientiane institution. It was run by a Frenchman called Maurice Cavalerie, a remarkable character with a fund of stories to entertain the few foreign correspondents who chose to cover the sideshow of the Laotian civil War rather than the bigger conflict of Vietnam, as well as occasional travellers such as myself.

. Cavalerie was born in Kunming in southern China in 1923 to a French father and a Chinese mother. He studied at the Lycée Albert Sarraut in Hanoi before enrolling in the medical faculty at the university there. As a side-line he started trading in sugar and other commodities that became scarce during the Second World War. When the Japanese, who had occupied Vietnam as part of their conquest of South East Asia, started to intern French nationals towards the end of the War, he went underground, until the arrival of the Nationalist Chinese army for whom he became an interpreter in their negotiations with the French authorities who were returning in the hope of restoring French colonial rule. Cavalerie was evacuated to France in 1946, but returned to Vietnam three years later, making a small fortune by supplying champagne, wines and gastronomic delicacies to the French community that was scattered across the country. However, the 1954 Geneva Accords, which brought an end to the first Indo-China War between Ho Chi Minh's forces and the French and divided Vietnam, awarded the North to the Communist Viet Minh. This meant that Cavalerie and his French wife and growing family had to abandon all their fixed assets and move south

163

to Dalat. Having decided that Laos was a marginally more secure long-term prospect than South Vietnam, he scouted out business opportunities in Vientiane before moving his family there and opening the Hotel Constellation. The best thing about the hotel as far many guests was concerned was the excellent French restaurant, with its respectable wine list, not that I was able to take advantage of that given my limited travel budget. The restaurant and bar moreover provided a centre for gossip and political intrigue among the journalists, diplomats, entrepreneurs and spies who gathered there, giving it the atmosphere of an Oriental equivalent of Rick Blaine's nightclub in Michel Curtiz's film *Casablanca*. Maurice Cavalerie silently observed everything going on until somebody inveigled him to talk about his youthful exploits. At the hotel reception desk one was able to change money at the black market rate, which was also used to calculate one's bill.

Vientiane's main street, the Avenue Lang Xang, was far too wide for the limited amount of traffic on it and it was decidedly fraying at the edges. At one end was a monstrous Arc de Triomphe known as the Patuxai. This was clearly based on the celebrated monument in Paris, despite Laotian design flourishes. At first I assumed that it was part of the French colonial legacy, until I realised that builders were still putting the finishing touches to it. In fact they had been working on it for the past decade, as a memorial to those who died in the war of liberation *against* the French. This seemed to be a strange extravagance given that Laos was economically in a pretty sorry state, largely relying on American aid for survival. There was very little of interest in the shops in Vientiane, practically all of which were owned by Chinese or Indians; the few imported goods were all very expensive.

The city nonetheless had two claims to fame at the time, firstly as a black market centre for gold and opium and secondly as being the only place in the world where one could find embassies of the United States, the Soviet Union, the People's Republic of China and the official governments of both North and South Vietnam. It struck me that the Laotians must be very tolerant to allow the North Vietnamese to maintain an embassy as North Vietnamese troops were fighting alongside Pathet Lao guerrillas in the northern provinces of Laos in their campaign to take over the country and to remove the King, who was based at the royal capital of Luang Prabang.

As there was a North Vietnamese Embassy in town I thought I would see if I could be any more successful with a visa application there than I had been in Phnom Penh. The Embassy was hidden away in a side street, but identifiable by the flag hanging outside, yet the first two times I went there no-one answered the bell. Only after a phone call did I ascertain that the building I had located was only an annex and that the entrance to the main building was around the corner, through big iron gates behind which several large dogs were prowling menacingly. A sour-faced little man accepted my passport when I passed it through the gates, telling him I wanted a visa, but when he returned a little while later he thrust it back at me together with a handwritten note saying I should return the following Monday. As I intended to be back in Thailand by then I had to accept that my ambition to see how the Communist North of Vietnam compared with the South was not going to be realised any time soon. The unfriendly reception from the official, who suddenly seemed to speak nothing but Vietnamese when I asked why my application could not be dealt with straight away, contrasted sharply with the courtesy of his counterpart in Phnom Penh, but this was possibly because in Vientiane all sorts of rumours were doing the rounds of North Vietnamese diplomats having been spotted digging a huge hole in the embassy's back garden. The speculation around the bar at the Hotel Constellation was that this was going to be an air-raid shelter in preparation for the day when MIG jets would arrive overhead to bomb Vientiane. Though there was little sign of War in the capital, the Pathet Lao rebels were said to have virtually surrounded Luang Prabang and a number of foreigners, mainly French missionaries and American Peace Corps workers, had been assassinated not far from Vientiane.

* * *

Back in Bangkok, the Burmese Embassy at first refused to issue my 24-hour transit visa unless I could prove that I was a student, not

165

a journalist. I had by now become quite adept at switching from one identity to the other, but at first they demanded that I hand over my NUS card for them to keep. Eventually I persuaded them to accept a photocopy, though it took me half an hour to find a shop in the neighbourhood that had a photocopier. It was a pleasant change when I called round to the Iranian embassy a few days later to find that they did not require a photo or even want me to fill in an application form but instead charged a fee of just 10 Thai baht for a visa to be stamped in my passport.

It was during this stay in Bangkok, during which Jeremy took me to see the city's historical sights, as well as making a day trip to Nakorn Pathom, that I decided to become a vegetarian. I had been scaling down my consumption of meat ever since my time working on the Ladywood by-election in Birmingham, but now I vowed to eschew all meat and fish, perhaps influenced by some of the Buddhists I had been meeting as well as a couple of vegetarian Quakers. As many Thais were seasonally vegetarian, in keeping with their Buddhist beliefs, in principle Thailand should have been one of the easiest countries in the world to make this shift, but as Jeremy mainly preferred to eat Western food I found myself surviving mainly on omelettes for a while as this was the only vegetarian option in the upmarket international restaurants he usually took me to, my favourite being at the Montien Hotel. I did not know that Harold had asked him to feed me up while I was in Bangkok and to send him the total bill. That I only discovered months later, back in Eccles, just before starting university, when Harold greeted me by holding out an itemised bill, declaring, 'You see how much you've cost me!'

* * *

There were not much more than a dozen passengers on the Union of Burma Airways flight to Rangoon, mainly Russians and Germans. One of the latter was someone I had spotted at Angkor Wat in Cambodia; a slightly spooky element of my travels from now on was the fact that I kept bumping into the same people as slowly I made my way across the land mass of Asia back to Europe. As the plane

166

came in to land at Rangoon the whole landscape below looked flooded from the monsoon. On the bus into the city a young Russian sitting next to me sighed deeply and declared how wonderful it was to be in such a lovely place compared with the Americanised vulgarity of Bangkok. Looking round at the dilapidated state of the colonial era buildings that we were passing, some of them green with mould, I wondered if he really believed what he was saying or whether he had been conditioned to trot out a Soviet line, especially in earshot of his compatriots, all of whom must have been Communist Party members or else at least were trusted by the apparatchiks in Moscow. Otherwise they would never have received passports that were valid outside the Soviet bloc. Burma itself was an uncompromisingly socialist state, still under the rule of General Ne Win, who held the position of Prime Minister as well as Chairman of the Union Revolutionary Council. He had seized power seven years previously in a military coup and oversaw the installation of a brand of socialism that was a curious concoction of Marxism, Buddhism and extreme nationalism. His Burma Socialist Programme Party was the only party permitted and it espoused a policy of autarchy or economic independence through self-sufficiency.

On arrival in Rangoon, I left my luggage at the Union of Burma Airways office and walked out of the centre of town towards the Shwedagon Pagoda. As the government had nationalised most sectors of the economy I passed remarkably few shops or other private businesses along the way. The side streets were lined with tumbledown terraced houses that looked as if nothing had been done to them for 30 or more years; only a few old cars moved slowly among all the bicycles along the tree-lined main road that was patchily surfaced, with an open sewer running down the side in places. The inhabitants, bulky black umbrellas hanging from their arms, were all wearing cloth *longyis* that looked drab and dirty compared with those of their Cambodian counterparts and people seemed astonished to see a European. Several of the cyclists stopped and dismounted to stare at this young white intruder, coldly and seemingly with mistrust. The only person who spoke to me was a black marketer hoping to buy US dollars. Yet as I approached the park by the Royal Lake near Singuttara Hill, the crowd thinned out and the atmosphere totally changed.

The Shwedagon stupa, said to have been founded 2,500 years ago and to contain strands of the Lord Buddha's hair and other holy relics, rises 300 feet above a platform and is visible from a long way off. You climb up a covered stairway to reach the platform, passing little stalls selling religious articles and beautiful flowers. At this point you must remove both shoes and socks. Arriving at the platform was the most moving sight I have ever seen. The gold-plated stupa allegedly crowned with diamonds rises proud from the marble courtyard and all around are shrines containing huge reclining Buddhas, gold images of many kinds and monks giving religious lessons. The twilight sky forms a magnificent celestial ceiling, the fading light reflected off a thousand mirrors twinkling round the shrines. The candles become brighter as the daylight fades. The air is heady with the scent of jasmine and the sound of gongs and soft chanting. Everywhere there are people deep in earnest prayer; others walk slowly and silently round the stupa, clockwise. It is the most spiritual place I have ever been to and I was in a daze as I followed the pilgrims in their circumambulation, drinking in the atmosphere. It is as if one is sharing a sacred mystery. I felt immensely privileged but also glad there were no other foreign visitors. Yet how can such a dismal city contain such a treasure and the people tolerate that paradox?

The street lighting in the suburbs was virtually non-existent but I managed to find my way back in the dark to the centre, where all the young men of Rangoon seemed to be queueing outside cinemas showing both Burmese and old American films. I had dinner at the Strand Hotel, a large colonial-style establishment almost devoid of guests apart from some of the transit passengers who had come in on my flight, though in the empty drawing room a band was playing Victorian popular tunes. As I had decided I could not afford the luxury of a night at the hotel I slept, surprisingly well, on a table in the Union of Burma Airways office under a mosquito net that the staff provided. They woke me at 5.30 the following morning so I could go round to the Strand Hotel to join the other passengers to catch the bus out to the airport. It was pouring with rain and after the plane took off it seemed to be making very slow progress until it suddenly descended for an unscheduled stop at Akyab on the coast near the border with East Pakistan (the future Bangladesh). The place looked half-deserted, its tiny airport hut lashed by the rain. It was a surreal scene, almost cinematic, and felt an appropriate end to my tantalising glimpse of Burma which had nonetheless been enough to whet my appetite for a longer exploratory visit one day when the country cast aside its paranoid fear of the outside world.

* * *

Our Burmese plane was met at Calcutta's Dum Dum airport by a fire engine squirting foam all over it as apparently one engine was about to burst into flames; it must have been the engine's overheating that caused the unexpected stop at Akyab. As the flight was so late arriving and passing through Indian Customs took an age, the Union of Burma Airways bus that should have ferried us passengers into the city had already given up and left. Three of us piled into a taxi along with a helpful young woman from the local tourist office and drove to the Red Shield Salvation Army Hostel in Sudder Street, where for 8 rupees a night I got a bed in a room for three, the other two boarders being a young American and an Indian student, both who had been living there for some time. The entrance to the hostel was thronged by groups of people wanting to change money, buy or sell things or simply begging. Beggars seemed to be everywhere in the filthy streets, many of them clearly living on the pavement, while cows wandered nonchalantly around snuffling in piles of garbage looking for something to eat. The poverty in Calcutta was so much worse than anything I had seen in South East Asia.

On the first evening, my new American room-mate introduced me to the nearby Hindustan Restaurant where there was a good selection of cheap vegetarian options, all of which appeared as a somewhat sloppy mess which had to be scooped up with pieces of naan. But the Salvation Army hostel resident with whom I developed a friendship that would last for many years was an intense but intelligent young Catholic woman from Paris, Marie-Louise Houlbert, who had come to India in search of some kind of spiritual enlightenment. She was relieved to find someone to whom she could talk to her in her own language, which she spoke at tremendous speed, as if all her thoughts had been bottled up inside her for weeks. She took me to the covered Hogg Market on Lindsay Street where I bought three metres of brocade for my sister Hilary. We then moved on to the nearby animal market that stank to high heaven but was filled with every conceivable type of bird as well as several species of animals. Along one side of the animal market was a hellish slum area comprised of mud-brick huts teaming with half-naked children. The unpaved alleyways were covered with human faeces, while mangy, almost hairless dogs lay asleep in the sun. Goats and carrion crows were picking at the piles of rubbish in competition with old women who were crouched on the ground carefully sifting through what other people had thrown away. Looking at Marie-Louise, I wondered aloud whether it was possible to find enlightenment among such degradation. Moreover, when I spoke later to an Indian businessman whose contact details I had been given in Saigon, he said the situation in Calcutta was deteriorating. He warned me that it would be dangerous for me to go into the poorer suburbs to take photographs, as I had wished, in order to pitch an article to the Geographical Magazine, as the situation was explosive. Protest demonstrations against the government in New Delhi were taking place daily, often with the covert support of Calcutta's Communist administration.

Another young Englishman at the hostel had recently arrived from the Nepalese capital, Kathmandu, and waxed lyrical about that city's beauty and serenity. Marie-Louise and I were of course aware that Kathmandu had the reputation of a Shangri La, to which hippies from all over Europe, North America and Australasia were flocking, in principle to meditate but in practice often to experiment with drugs. The hippie movement had begun in the United States, developing a kind of alternative philosophy and lifestyle that was rooted in harmony with nature, communal living, sexual freedom and artistic experimentation. By the late 1960s it had also become a safe space for young Americans who were opposed to the Vietnam War. One of its core slogans was 'Make Love, Not War'. Another was

170

'Let a thousand parks bloom', which was a play on Mao Zedong's declaration in 1957 that 'to let a hundred flowers blossom and a hundred schools of thought contend is the policy for promoting progress in the arts and the sciences and a flourishing socialist culture in our land'. The parks reference in the hippies' version related to the People's Park that students and local residents had established at Berkeley, California, in April 1969. Weeks later, as I had learned while I was in Okinawa, the Governor of California, Ronald Reagan, had ordered the occupation of Berkeley by the US National Guard. This prompted a campaign of Gandhian civil disobedience by the hippies who planted flowers on vacant lots that were due for redevelopment. The concept of flower power was thus born. While I was in South Asia the Woodstock Festival took place in Bethel, New York, where half a million people gathered to celebrate this new counter-culture, with musical performances by Joan Baez, Janis Joplin, Jimi Hendrix and others. I only heard about that when I returned to England, but I did know that in February 1968 The Beatles had gone to Rishikesh in northern India to attend an advanced course in Transcendental Meditation with their guru, Maharishi Mahesh Yogi. This had proved to be something of a disaster, not least because of rumours of inappropriate behaviour and financial irregularities on the part of the Maharishi. Accordingly, Marie-Louise and I decided that we were more likely to find some sort of spiritual guidance in Nepal, rather than in India. We agreed we would both therefore head for Kathmandu, though making our separate ways there.

The following morning I woke to torrential rain that had turned to streets of Calcutta into rivers. Local men rolled up their trousers or dhotis to pick their way gingerly through the swirling water, but one of the rough sleepers outside the hostel had obviously died in the night as his emaciated body was just bobbing gently up and down, waiting for someone to take him away. Gingerly I made my way through Chowringhee to the Indian railway offices to apply for a student concession travel permit. India was famed as the largest and most cumbersome bureaucracy in the world and when I finally located the right office I found a middle-aged man sitting in front of a desk that was piled high with dusty paper files. The official was

171

polite but worked with the lethargy of a man paid very little to do essentially mind-numbing tasks yet enjoying the little bit of power that he had at his disposal in granting or not granting the necessary piece of paper or stamp to supplicants. As his hands moved methodically from one file to another, or to fish some item of stationery from a drawer, like some ancient clockwork machine, there was a barely discernible smile on his face and his eyes were vacant as if his mind was far away. Sitting for hours in offices in Vietnam had taught me the virtue of patience, so I remained silent on the rickety wooden chair in front of his desk until he satisfied himself that everything was in order and I emerged triumphantly with my concession pass. This gave a 50% reduction on train fares all the way across the country. At another office I was then able to purchase a ticket to Raxaul in Bihar state, the major crossing point for road traffic into Nepal.

On the afternoon of my departure, another student from the hostel and I got a taxi to the giant Howrah railway station on the west bank of the Hooghly River. The vehicle inched its way across the Howrah Bridge, which was thronged by thousands of people pushing animals and carts, causing a massive traffic jam. They looked more like refugees fleeing a war than people going about their daily business. At the station itself, hundreds of people had made the building their home, their few possessions piled on the floor beside them or else under the heads as they slept. One emaciated old man was completely naked, his bones sticking out through his skin, and the resigned look on his face of an animal that was preparing to die. It was a relief to get on the train and I was glad I had booked a first-class sleeper ticket (with the 50% student discount) as although the compartment was old and dirty it had its own private toilet, a lockable door and bars over the window, to stop other people trying to climb in, as they were doing in the jam-packed third class carriages further along the train. Our compartment was for four people only and I was relieved that my new travelling companions, all Indian, were not particularly talkative, once they had trotted out the inevitable question, 'Where are you coming from?' They had all brought bulky bed-rolls with them, so turning their couchettes into comfortable beds. As the train progressed slowly through the evening

172

and night towards Samastipur in Bihar state it was possible to buy tea and snacks from vendors on the platforms of the stations where it stopped.

I was woken at 4am the following morning by one of my fellow-passenger's singing. At least that meant I was wide awake and ready to change trains when we pulled into Samastipur an hour or so later. The connection was smooth onto a train heading for Raxaul on the Nepalese frontier. This took about seven hours, travelling past mile after mile of fields planted with maize. The houses in the villages we passed were largely made of brick, with thatched rooves, while along the earth roads farmers coaxed fat buffaloes along with rods. It was a blessing to be out of the tropics, as the dry heat of Bihar was much easier to bear than the sweaty monsoon of Calcutta, especially when a breeze blew in through the open carriage window. Among the other passengers on the train was an earnest young missionary couple from Sheffield who were travelling third class with their baby. I thought wistfully of my childhood ambition to be a Christian missionary in India. I had never returned to talk to the Bishop of Middleton, Ted Wickham, about this, as by the time I was old enough to consider training for the priesthood I had lost my faith in the Church of England. Indeed, now I was in South Asia, far from wanting to convert the 'natives' – as they were often still referred to by Britons in the 1960s – I was ready to learn from them.

* * *

I hired a horse-cart to take me from Raxaul station to the border post, where an Indian Customs officer checked my currency declaration form, yet did not seem bothered that the figures on it did not quite correspond to the money I had with me. I looked up to the Himalayan mountains that were now clearly in sight and heaved a sigh of relief. On the Nepalese side of the border, the immigration officer at first refused to believe that my visa was genuine as he had not heard about the new Nepalese Embassy opening in Bangkok, but eventually he believed me and I was able to walk into the village of Birgunj. This consisted of little more than one main street, where I checked into the Deluxe Lodge, which despite its name charged less than three Indian rupees a night.

The road from Birgunj to Kathmandu was known as the Rajpath and had only been built in the 1950s; it was narrow but well-surfaced, except where landslides had carried some of it away. Prior to its construction (by the Indians, who were hoping to prevent Nepal from cementing too close links with China), people wanting to travel into Nepal from India had to take a narrow-gauge railway from Raxaul to Amlekhganj, where they then had to mount elephants to take them to Hetauda, from which sedan chairs and donkeys were available for them to proceed to Kathmandu. The fact that the Kingdom of Nepal had largely cut itself off from the outside world for several years after the Second World War had only heightened its isolation.

The bus ride from Birgunj to Kathmandu was exhilarating for its scenery, even though the higher peaks were hidden above the clouds. Because of my physical size and nationality, the driver insisted I sit next to him, which gave me a brilliant viewpoint, though the heat from the engine almost melted my flipflops. It took 11 hours – with numerous stops for tea – to climb the mountain range to a height of 8,000 feet before descending into the Kathmandu valley. We passed several Soviet-sponsored aid projects along the way. Nepal might be one of the poorest countries on earth but it was learning how to attract development assistance from major donors everywhere, East and West. At one point the bus had to cross a narrow iron bridge where a group of village children were standing holding a rope across the road and demanding money as a 'toll', but the 'hold-up' was fairly good-natured and the children did not seem too surprised or disappointed when the bus-driver just carried on. Apparently it was National Beggars Day, when it is alright in Nepalese culture for the needy, including children, to ask for alms (though not at other times). Perhaps they would have more luck with cars or jeeps crossing the bridge, though we saw hardly any of those on the road. At the entrance to Kathmandu there was a customs post – a wooden hut inside which a lone man was sitting at an old table, the only light coming from a single candle. Like the immigration at Birgunj he did not recognise the visa I had acquired in Bangkok, but when I agreed to fill out another form he let me through.

At the bus terminus in Kathmandu a tout persuaded me to accompany him to the Travellers Lodge, a cheap but clean boarding house in the Jochen district of the old city, just south of Durbar Square. For the next couple of weeks I shared a room there with a young Indian called Gupta, who described himself as a pharmaceutical salesman; it soon became evident, from the stream of young Western visitors to our room over the following days, that he was actually a black marketeer, supplying everything from contraceptive pills to morphine. No wonder the nickname for this area among young travellers was Freak Street. Yet there was a curious air of innocence about the place, underlined at the Lodge by an eager 15-year-old Nepali tea-boy called Lollipop who ran errands whenever asked.

I had no intention of experimenting with any of Gupta's wares but I fell immediately under Kathmandu's spell. The city was only a fraction of its present size – fewer than 200,000 people – and almost devoid of motor traffic. The narrow streets of the city centre wound among old wooden houses, a few bicycles and rickshaws moving with difficulty through the throngs of people, the cows and the goats. There were lots of tiny little shops selling Nepalese and Tibetan handicrafts, as well as cafés and restaurants catering mainly to the young Western travellers. One reason the place was so popular with the hippies was that it was extraordinarily cheap. It was possible to rent a bed in a dormitory for under 2 US dollars a month and to eat for just a few cents, which is how many of the hippies and drop-outs managed to survive there for months, even years, though many got sick from the water or the food or from infected needles, if they were drug-users. Apart from diarrhoea and stomach upsets, the major health concern was hepatitis, which was cutting a swathe through the travellers. Accordingly almost the first thing I did in Kathmandu was to go to a clinic to get a jab of gamma globulin in my hip.

That very first day out on the streets in Kathmandu I ran into Marie-Louise Houlbert, who had already discovered some of the best places to eat. One that soon became a favourite was Tashi's, which was run by a sweet, gentle Tibetan and his son, both with wizened,

175

dark mongoloid faces and knowing black eyes. Tibetans seemed to have cornered the market in creating spaces where young Europeans and Americans liked to hang out, the most celebrated example being a noodle-shop called the Tibetan Blue, named after a type of mountain bear, but invariably referred to by its Western customers as the Blue Tibetan because of the restaurant's blue walls. Originally it had served Tibetan muleteers, but the hippies soon took over, the men usually bearded and often in South Asian robes, the girls in long flowery dresses. You could get a buffalo steak and a big pile of Tibetan bread, all washed down with tea, for 30 US cents. However, the serious drug-addicts preferred the Cabin Restaurant, which was located up a dirty little alley and specialised in Hash Cookies and other dishes or drinks laced with marijuana or other drugs. It had only been open a few months but already looked seedy; on the wall was a poster proclaiming 'Keep the World Beautiful – Stay Stoned'. The air was full of the aroma of *charas*, a hand-made form of hashish made from the resin of the cannabis plant, and the latest Western music belting out from the stereo system made conversation difficult. When I went into the Cabin with Marie-Louise, who often dressed as if she was on her way to church, we were met by what seemed like dozens of bleary, stoned, even fearful eyes. It was obvious to everyone that we didn't fit in, so we soon left.

The next morning the two of us hired bicycles and cycled out along the Kathmandu Valley to the ancient Newar town of Badgaon, also known as Bhaktapur or Place of the Devotees, about 14 kilometres from the capital. I thought it was the most sublime town I had ever visited. In its Durbar Square a central Palace of 55 Windows built in brick and timber was surrounded by a conglomeration of temples and pagodas, most dedicated to Hindu deities. Many of the local people as well as visiting pilgrims were making offerings at different shrines, while others went about their daily tasks. They seemed curious to see two young Europeans in their midst, but friendly in a restrained way. No-one here, or in Kathmandu, pestered one for money or other help, in stark contrast to the situation in Calcutta. Yet when I walked up in the hills beyond town one afternoon, an old man came chasing after me, playing a stringed instrument like a tiny violin, which he was hoping I would

176

buy. He was only asking the equivalent of a pound for it but it looked like a family heirloom, perhaps even old enough to fall foul of the country's law against the export of antiques. I repeatedly demurred until eventually he stopped following me and stood forlornly, the instrument now held soundless in one hand dangling by his side, looking after me with immeasurably sad eyes.

* * *

Last night I dreamt I was circulating the Nyatapola Temple in Badgaon, silently chanting a mantra I can no longer remember. Then I saw a European woman of about 40 mounting the steps. I stopped to look at her receding back and thought that she must be English. Unlike the hippies from America or Australia, in their long, loose-fitting flowery dresses, she was wearing the sort of fashionable above-the-knee frock of Swinging Sixties London I knew from magazines, and her hair was in a half-beehive. Suddenly I realised that this was no stranger. This was my mother. I started to follow her up the steps of the pagoda but my mouth was dry and I could not call out to her, no matter how hard I tried. Nor could I walk faster, in order to catch up with her. I reached one arm out but could not touch her. The steps went on and on upwards, well past the five stories of the pagoda in real life. Then she arrived at an open platform at the top, where she turned. But where her face should have been, there was just a white blank. And she made not a sound before disappearing into the void.

I woke, sweating and deflated, with a terrible feeling of emptiness and loss gnawing at the pit of my stomach. I wanted to return to sleep and to plunge back into my dream and to keep following her until she recognised me and stopped.

* * *

As I was lingering in Nepal, I decided I had better do something useful, in other words some work that would earn me some money when I got back to England. I thought I might be able to sell a piece to the Geographical Magazine on the diversity of foreign aid to

177

Nepal, so over the next few days I did the rounds of several of the major embassies in Kathmandu to collect material: the Russians, the Chinese, the Japanese, the Israelis, the Germans, the French and the British. The last was housed in a large compound where several of the diplomats also lived and one of them, Duncan Spain, invited me round for dinner at his house there a few days later. I had no jacket to wear for that, but borrowed a pair of decent dark trousers from one of my fellow guests at the Lodge and had my one short-sleeved white shirt cleaned and ironed at a laundry. I was still seriously under-dressed compared with the other guests, who included the Nepalese Minister of the Economy, Nepal's newly-appointed Ambassador to Japan and the American Ambassador's wife. Fortunately they treated me indulgently as some sort of youthful curiosity, quizzing me in particular about my journey across the USSR on the Trans-Siberian railway.

Through the Israeli mission I got an introduction to the Ministry of Agriculture, where I sat in on an extraordinary meeting at which an engineer from Switzerland was trying to finalise arrangements for the construction of a factory to make cornflakes. It struck me as odd that a country as poor as Nepal would have sufficient demand for breakfast cereal, but the man from the Ministry declared cheerily that 'the potential market for cornflakes in Nepal is *huge!*' However, the Swiss engineer was making little progress with the Nepalese as they seemed to have no relevant statistics of agricultural production available. When he asked about the size of the maize crop, the agricultural chief beamed and said emphatically, 'Lots!' I found it hard to keep a straight face, particularly as the Swiss man was looking increasingly frustrated. I went away afterwards realising that alas there was insufficient material for a magazine article in all this, though the meeting at the Ministry might make a good scene for a comic novel.

The weather that had been blissful up until then suddenly broke and for several days there was torrential rain which turned Kathmandu's unmade roads into a quagmire. Having stayed longer in Nepal than I had originally intended, I decided to catch up on my travel schedule by taking an Indian Airlines flight from Kathmandu to Benares rather than making the time-consuming journey overland.

178

Kathmandu airport was in a shambles when I got there, partly because it was being extended and modernised but mainly because of the havoc caused by the weather. Although the rain had by now stopped in Kathmandu there was reportedly heavy flooding in northern India. Some people had been sitting around at the airport for a week waiting for a flight to Delhi. My flight was delayed by several hours because of floods in Benares but just as we passengers were sitting down to lunch provided by Indian Airlines a steward came running to say the plane was about to take off, causing a stampede to the departure gate. The Fokker Friendship plane was full and flew quite low over the mountains but the heavy cloud cover meant there was no chance of catching a glimpse of Everest or any of the other high Himalayan peaks.

* * *

As the plane came into land at Benares the whole landscape seemed to be under water. I had linked up with a young Canadian called Chuck on the flight and together we made our way to the Dak bungalow that was located in a large park boasting magnificent trees at the back of the Hotel de Paris, and which had been recommended as a good but reasonably priced place to stay. Oddly, both the Dak bungalow and the hotel were almost empty of guests, but the meals served at the latter for anyone who cared to eat there were enormous.

The rain had abated so the following afternoon under a bright blue sky we got a pedicab downtown to see the River Ganges. This had swelled to twice its normal size, covering many of the ghats where bodies were normally cremated. The water was a raging torrent almost two miles wide and hundreds of people were milling round aimlessly, frustrated at not being able to bathe safely in the sacred water. The next day we accepted the offer from a little Indian boy who came up to us in the street to be our guide for the day for the princely sum of one rupee. This proved to be a worthwhile investment, as he was able to lead us through a maze of alleyways to a building from whose roof we got an excellent view of the golden Kashi Vishwanath temple. The temple itself was closed to non-Hindus, but later in another alley we were able to get a glimpse of

179

the interior of the temple through a side window. Having failed to tempt us to buy some brasswork from a nearby shop where he knew the owner, our little guide then took us to the Nepalese Temple which, like the Golden Temple, was dedicated to Lord Shiva but built in terracotta, stone and wood Nepalese style – in fact it was a copy of the Pashupatinath Temple in Kathmandu. The little boy was especially keen to show us the erotic wood carvings in a section protected behind bars, which allegedly illustrate positions from the Kama Sutra.

Just a stone's throw from these symbols of fertility and human reproduction was the Manikarnika Burning Ghat, which we accessed across a muddy beach where half-naked woodcutters were chopping logs for the fires that burn the dead bodies. The air was filled with the sound of the chopping, the smoke from the fires creating a haze, and a strange, almost sweet smell of burning flesh. To one side were two bodies wrapped in cloth and soaked after a final dip in the Ganges. Dotted around on little pyres lay half-consumed corpses that were burning extremely slowly; they were still in recognisable human form, yet in reality were nothing more than empty shells. On the way to the Ghat I had wondered how I would feel about this spectacle but in fact it seemed little more than the sanitary disposal of waste matter. The heads of the adult corpses did not burn but were thrown into the river, as were the bodies of small children. As Chuck, our boy guide and I rowed away in a little boat, the whole scene, with the beautiful jumble of temples and buildings behind, seemed as unreal as a dream. It was strictly forbidden to take photographs, but I knew that this was one image that would stick in my mind for the rest of my life.

* * *

An overnight train transported me from Benares to Agra with a connection at Tundla Junction, so I arrived at the Agra tourist bungalow in time for a quick breakfast and a shower before heading off in a pedicab for the Taj Mahal, where I had a rendezvous with Chuck, who had made the journey from Benares by air.

The Taj is quite a way out of town, driving past a very fine fort and along a tree-lined avenue. As one goes in through the gates the view of the Taj is hidden until one is under the main entrance and then wham! Hit like a thunderbolt you stare, heart missing a beat. Colossal it stands, so white, so perfect. Here is indeed the jewel of India mounted on a precious setting. The shutter clicks, but the camera can never capture the sheer size or the atmosphere of the place. The façade of the Taj is a delicate work that is almost a paradox given the building's volume. Inside, enclosed by a finely-carved marble lattice screen is a replica of the Queen's tomb, while below lies the real thing in a vault, with the King's – larger and off-centre – beside.

In the evening Chuck and I return, fortunate that this is the night before the full moon. The avenue is sparkling with the lights of fire-flies and the Taj stands eerie as a frozen block, quite different from the daytime palace, now truly a tomb. It glows faintly in the strong moonlight, which casts long shadows at your feet. This is beauty again but a sinister beauty. I wonder how the planned Black Taj would have looked on the other side of the river, but am glad it was never built to mimic perfection. I am also glad Chuck is here as one needs someone to share the feeling generated by such wonderful sights.

* * *

At the next stop on my journey home, Delhi, having bid farewell to Chuck, I went to the Post Office to see what letters they were holding for me at the Poste Restante. To my amazement, among them was one from the office of the President of Syria, forwarded from Eccles. I had completely forgotten about the rather peevish missive I had sent to Nureddin al-Atassi, complaining about the fact that his country would not give a visa to an English schoolboy, but here was an extremely courteous response from his secretariat saying that I would be very welcome to visit Syria whenever I wished. I had previously planned a more northerly route back to Europe via Iran and South East Turkey but this seemed too good an opportunity to miss. Fortunately, in keeping with India's Non-Aligned status, there

181

was a Syrian Embassy in New Delhi. When I arrived there and said I had to come to apply for a tourist visa the man at the reception was about to tell me that would not be possible when I pulled out my letter from Damascus. The expression on his face changed immediately and I was then ushered into a room where I was served coffee and dates while I handed over my passport into which a visa was duly stamped.

As the UK and Syria still did not have diplomatic relations, I thought I had better go to the British High Commission, which was conveniently located nearby, just to find out which country had agreed to look after British subjects' interests in the absence of a British Embassy. This turned out to be Switzerland, but the young diplomat at the High Commission who unearthed this information warned me strongly against going to Syria as tensions were still high in the Middle East following Israel's occupation of the Golan Heights as well as the West Bank and Gaza. I told him that as I had survived the Vietnam War I was sure I could manage in the Middle East. Standing up and holding himself erect, so as to emphasize the gravity of what he was about to say, on behalf of Her Majesty's Government, he declared slowly, 'Well, don't say I haven't warned you!'

* * *

Today, Wednesday 27 August, 1969, Harold turns 68 and it's the first time ever I haven't had to be with him on his birthday. But last night I had a nightmare in which I was suddenly transported back to Eccles, having cashed in my remaining traveller's cheques and bought an air-ticket all the way 'home'. At Manchester Ringway Airport, Harold was there waiting for me, alone and angry. Very angry. He accused me of having cut and run, of having failed and brought shame on him. I had said I would go to Vietnam and back overland, as much as was possible. And now I had let him down. He had been getting his old secretary at Fryer's to type out copies of the letters I have been sending ever since Japan and circulating them among his pals at the Worsley Golf Club. 'And now you have given

182

up and just come back,' he said. 'How could you humiliate me like that?'

I woke up in a sweat and just wanted to disappear through the damp sheet and the bed and the floor into nothingness. I seem to be crushed under a great weight and can see no way out. And now I am afraid to go to sleep again, in case that dream returns.

* * *

Harold's 68th birthday was the last day I wrote an entry in my diary until more than two years later. I had not been feeling physically very well since I had left Kathmandu and I found the intense heat of Delhi oppressive. But that was not the reason I stopped writing. The nightmare, which would repeat itself insistently over the coming weeks, like a sledgehammer breaking down a wall, had profoundly unsettled my mind. Though of course I knew I hated Harold for years I had not yet been able to come to terms with *why*. Standing by the lake at Dalat, earlier in the summer, I had caught a glimpse of what was stored in the deepest recesses of my memory, behind a mass of cotton wool, but I had hastily pushed it back. Now I could no longer do so, and vivid recollections of the fear and nausea associated with Harold's visits to the room over the garage during my childhood were now demanding my attention. I was overcome with dizziness as they crowded through to the front of my consciousness as I sat drinking a pot of milky tea at a café in Delhi's Connaught Circus. The thought that every step I now took for the rest of this journey would bring me closer to Harold and to Eccles made me feel positively sick, but I told myself that I must hang on to my sanity without breaking down, as in the autumn I would be going to Oxford and after that a new life lay ahead.

As it happens, I had indeed been concerned that I might have to fly at least part of the way back to England, as the border between India and West Pakistan was often closed and the Iranians had closed their frontier with Afghanistan because of a cholera outbreak, leaving several hundred overland travellers stranded in Herat. I went to the Aeroflot airline office in Delhi where I discovered that they were offering a flight from Delhi to Bucharest via Tashkent and Moscow

183

at the student rate of US$230, including an overnight stay in the Soviet capital. However, when I called at the Pakistan High Commission to apply for a route permit to cross into their country a very friendly and obliging official assured me that with that permit and my British passport I would have no problem entering his country, so I decided to press ahead. I made sure that I saw the India Museum, the Red Fort and other major sights before I left Delhi, then I handed myself over to the railway system once again to get me to Ferozepur in Indian Punjab. There I got a pedicab to the village of Hussainiwalla, from where I had to walk on foot with my luggage through a wide no man's land, before finding a pedicab on the Pakistani side that would take me to the railway junction at Kasur. When the train for Peshawar in the North West Frontier Province arrived it was so full that I had to throw my little blue suitcase through a window and climb in after it, South Asian style. It was so hot in the packed third class carriage that I spent a lot of the journey north sitting on the steps of the carriage with a group of local boys, to catch the breeze. Almost all the passengers were male and dressed in the traditional *salwar kameez*; I was very much a curiosity and one old man pinched my pink cheeks to the merriment of our fellow passengers, several of whom insisted on pressing food on me as the journey progressed.

Peshawar was a wild and wonderful town inhabited mainly by Pashtun and other tribal people, many of whom sported beards and wore strands of bullets across their chests and a rifle over one shoulder, making them look fearsome, yet their warlike image was undermined by the fact that several of the men wore a flower behind one ear. Their gaze was direct and probing but not unfriendly. When I went to a barber's to have my long blondish hair cut the establishment was mobbed by curious onlookers, though to the barber's dismay, as well as mine, great clumps of hair came out when he first combed it. This had happened to me once before, when I was in Birmingham, working on the Ladywood by-election. On that occasion this had prompted me to seek an appointment with an anti-hair-loss centre, where I was told I would probably go bald by the time I was 30; not having any idea who my father was, I could not answer their question about whether there was a history of baldness

184

in the family. The barber in Peshawar gave me no such interrogation but I vowed from then on to keep my hair short, and bizarrely later my hairline stopped receding all of its own accord.

The main reason I had my hair shorn in Peshawar, apart from short hair being more comfortable in great heat, was to look as respectable as possible when I went to the Afghan Consulate to obtain a visa. I had tried to get one at the Afghan Embassy in New Delhi but had been told an overland entry permit would only be available in Peshawar. So I located the Consulate, which was on the second floor of a rather tatty office block, and went along dressed in my one white shirt and the beige linen slacks. All the way up the stairs from the entrance to the building snaked a harlequinade line of hippies, presumably returning home from Kathmandu or from Indian ashrams, most of them long-haired and dressed in a colourful medley of Oriental fabrics and copious amounts of beads, bangles and other adornments. I plonked myself at the end of the line, resigned for a long wait, but after a few minutes a Consulate employee came into the building from the street, took one look at me and then led me by the arm upstairs, past all the lounging hippies, right to the front of the queue, where he instructed an underling at the desk to put a visa in my passport immediately. The moral of this story, that would prove useful in later life, was that particularly in poor countries people respect those who are clean and dressed 'properly'.

The bus station at Peshawar was home to a motley collection of battered coaches with large roof-racks and even the odd double-decker bus, which must have been shipped out from England. The dirty white single-decker bus that wound its way up the Khyber Pass en route for Afghanistan left early in the morning and was packed with people, plus a mountain of luggage on the roof. As the gradient increased the engine groaned louder and every time the driver changed gear there was a terrible grinding noise. At times the narrow road clung precariously to the side of mountains and down in the valleys were carcasses of buses and trucks that had come off the road and plunged people to their deaths. As had happened before on my travels, as a courtesy as well as in recognition of my height, the driver insisted that I sit in the front next to him, which gave me a wonderful view of the scenery (bone dry and with almost no

185

vegetation) but also an unnerving close-up of oncoming traffic. There were several old forts and gun emplacements along the route, but the only time we stopped before crossing the frontier into Afghanistan and heading for Jalalabad was when prayer-time arrived and all the men poured off the bus with their mats to pray by the side of the road. Every so often we would pass small pick-up trucks which were full of standing men in turbans or embroidered caps, plus several others precariously balanced on the rear mudguard.

It was dark by the time we arrived in the Afghan capital, Kabul, and as the bus pulled into the terminus it was surrounded by touts sent by local hotels and hostels. As I was the only Westerner who disembarked I was immediately accosted by three or four young men each proclaiming in broken English the advantages of their particular establishment. I decided to hand myself over to the one who was cleanest, in the hope that his appearance was indicative of the state of his hostel, which did indeed prove to be the case. Not for the first time I had been lucky and after a quick meal in a nearby café I collapsed onto the bed in the room that I would be sharing with two local men and fell fast asleep.

When I woke in the morning I could feel a pair of eyes on me and sure enough, sitting on one of the other beds was a middle-aged Afghan man who was just watching me, motionless. When I sat up he smiled, a teeth-cleaning twig protruding from the side of his mouth, and he said *assalamualaikum*. I mumbled a response and as he was showing no signs of moving I got up wearing just my underpants and picked my other clothes up from the floor. He continued to watch as fascinated as if he was looking at a strange creature in a zoo. He nodded slightly after I had dressed and headed for the door, his curiosity apparently satisfied.

Kabul in 1969 was a great crossroads of cultures and peoples, vibrant and exotic. Women in modern dresses copied from French and Italian magazines walked alongside more traditional ladies who were completely hidden under pale blue burkas, their faces invisible behind the meshing. Everywhere people were selling things, from hole-in-the-wall shops to large, open markets and individuals who had spread out a few meagre offerings on a piece of cloth on the pavement. From one of the latter I bought an English translation of one of the seminal works of Lenin for the equivalent of 10 US cents. With hindsight, I cannot imagine why I wanted it, but I did faithfully carry it all the way back to England. There was plenty of street food on offer, too, though for a new convert to vegetarianism there was little that was appropriate; kebabs and other roast meat were the order of the day. However, carts piled high with strawberries brought in from the surrounding countryside were tempting. I found a cheap restaurant that served delicious strawberry cake, as well as rice cooked with various dried fruits and nuts.

Nonetheless I was getting noticeably thinner and suddenly I felt all my energy dissipate. I stayed in bed for several days, feeling drained and consuming almost nothing except the cups of tea that a concerned bearer at the hostel brought every hour or so while I tried to read back issues of the English-language Kabul Times. It was only when I got back to England that a blood test showed that I had had a mild dose of hepatitis. It would probably have been much worse had I not had the gamma globulin injection in Kathmandu, though I suspected I might actually have caught the infection from that needle, as the glass syringes had been used over and over again and the sterilisation facilities were basic.

Time was pressing, though, as I had to be back in England by early October in order to start my studies at St Edmund Hall. So as soon as I felt able to get up and walk I went down to the bus station in Kabul to catch a bus to Kandahar. The journey took all day, but even in my weakened state I savoured the magnificent landscape. The road followed the line of an immense, wide valley, while in the distance, mountains reared up on both sides. Somewhere beyond hills to the north were the famous Buddhas of Bamayan, and I regretted that I did not have the time to take a detour to see them. It was night-time when the bus pulled into Kandahar and as in Kabul, as I walked down the steps I was besieged by touts from local guest-houses. Once again I was lucky in the one I chose, though I like to think that maybe all the accommodation touts were fundamentally honest and their hostels equally welcoming.

There were several young Europeans and Australians at the hostel when I arrived and they were deep in conversation about the cholera outbreak in western Afghanistan. They confirmed what I had heard earlier that the Iranians had shut the border, which meant that all the accommodation in Herat was full of people who had had to halt their westward travel, while at the border itself there was a tented camp where the risk of infection, not just from cholera, was obvious. Most of the overlanders at the hostel were genuinely travelling on a shoe-string budget, but at least they had plenty of time, so they could afford to linger, though it seemed unlikely that the situation would improve any time soon. Several were enjoying the drugs that were easily available and cheap, though Kandahar as a city struck me as far more conservative than Kabul. Almost everyone in the streets was male and the few women one did see scurrying into their houses were invariably wearing burkas. Almost all the buildings were single-storey and there were far fewer goods on offer than in the capital. However, as I was walking along the main street I was astonished to see in the window of one shop a Pan American Airways poster promoting vacations in the United States. Intrigued, I went inside and discovered that this was a travel agent's and that there was a weekly Pan Am flight between South East Asia and the Middle East that stopped at both Kandahar and Tehran. Kandahar airport had been built by the Americans mainly as a refuelling station and it had only opened in 1962. Here was my lifeline, so I duly bought a ticket and a couple of days later was flying over Herat and the Iranian border, heading for Tehran. The PanAm stewardess was so concerned by my by now seriously skinny body and jaundiced face that she insisted I have two of the on board meals.

* * *

Tehran in the late 1960s, like Istanbul, was only a fraction of its current size. It was still essentially a low-rise city, though one that was modernising fast. The Shah, who had come to power in 1941 when the British ousted his pro-German father, crowned himself as King of Kings in a lavish ceremony in 1967, seemingly unaware that a sizeable part of the Iranian population was becoming increasingly unhappy with the way that he was Westernising Persia (as most people in Britain still called Iran). In the affluent suburbs of North Tehran one could see women who would not be out of place on the

188

Champs Élysées in Paris, but much of the rest of the country was socially and religiously conservative. The Shia Islamic hierarchy in Qom were vehemently opposed to the direction in which the Shah was steering the country and said so. In 1963 the Shah had launched what he called the White Revolution: a six-point plan which he believed could kick-start the country along the road to modernisation. This involved land reform, the privatisation of state-owned companies, the nationalization of forests, profit-sharing in companies, the enfranchisement of women and a massive campaign against illiteracy. Though hailed in the West as visionary, this White Revolution was denounced by the senior clerics, notably the Ayatollah Ruholla Khomeini, who particularly objected to what he saw as an un-Islamic change to the status of women. After a series of confrontations with the government, Khomeini was sent into exile in 1964, settling in Najaf, in neighbouring Iraq, the following year.

It was therefore not surprising that I sensed a somewhat strained atmosphere in Tehran. Only a small percentage of the Iranian population had benefited from the riches brought into the country's coffers by oil, and the mass of the population, even in Tehran, were clearly struggling to make ends meet, while a wealthy élite flaunted their Americanised lifestyle, driving round in sports cars and going to nightspots such as the 007 Psychadelic Club, where Western pop groups were sometimes invited over to play.

I had no introductions to anyone in the city. I suppose I could have gone to the British Embassy to make some contacts, but I was still feeling quite weak and lethargic and I was starting to sink into the sort of depression that I had experienced as a child. The nightmare about arriving back in England early to be met by Harold's wrath was still recurring, but now it alternated with a new dream in which Harold's hand, severed from his body but moving independently like a giant pink hermit crab that had lost its shell, kept coming towards me. In my dream I stabbed it repeatedly with a dinner fork, but this seemed to have no effect. Eventually the hand would reach my groin and I would wake up riven with anxiety. This left me with no motivation to explore Tehran, so I just frequented some of the numerous tea-shops and small cafés in the downtown area, where workmen and office workers viewed me slightly quizzically but left me to my own devices. I found myself dragging a teaspoon back and forth across table tops, mimicking the movement I had made with pencil points along the grooves of the wooden desks in junior classes at MGS. In the Tehran cafés there were trays of sweet *poolaki* and *nazook*, saffron candy and walnut rolled pastry. But these could not satisfy a sudden craving that I had – a craving for Eccles cakes. I was the little boy sitting in the graveyard at Eccles Parish Church again, the rain dripping down my face, as I slowly munched the raison and citrus peel and flaky pastry, deriving comfort from each mouthful. I sat silently in the Tehran cafés for hours, unable to move.

The one unavoidable decision I had to take, nonetheless, was which route I would follow to move on to Syria. The most logical seemed to be through Iraq and Jordan, but tension between Iran and Iraq had been a feature of the region ever since the British installed the Hashemite emir Faisal on the throne in Baghdad way back in 1921. The July 1968 Ba'athist coup d'état in Iraq, led by Ahmed Hassan al-Bakr and Saddam Hussein, had brought relations to a new low, yet I heard from other travellers at the hostel I was staying at in Tehran that the border between the two countries had recently re-opened, mainly to let Shia pilgrims from Iran travel to the holy cities of Najaf and Karbala.

Enquiring at the main bus station I discovered that there was an overnight coach that covered the whole journey of around 900 kilometres from Tehran to Baghdad via Qom and Kermanshah. The vehicles used were brand new and had reclining seats – much more comfortable than any bus I had travelled on so far. I booked a ticket for the following day's departure, choosing an aisle seat so I would be able to stretch out my legs if necessary. It was still light when we departed Tehran and drove off the main highway to Qom. I had heard that Westerners tended to receive a cool reception in that centre of Shia conservatism and it was noticeable that not only were all the few women in the streets here were wearing black *chadoors* but most of the men were dressed in clerical garb, being mullahs or students at the city's numerous madrassas. In contrast, the man sitting next to me on the coach, as I now noticed as I slightly leant over him to get a better view out of the window, was kitted out in baggy white cotton trousers with a matching long shirt out of which protruded two slender, extremely hirsute arms.

I had not taken much notice of him when I had boarded the bus, still being wrapped up in my own thoughts. I was conscious that I was the only foreigner on the bus and I had started to slip into the state of semi-meditation in which I had passed most the long road journeys so far. But at Qom the man smiled and said something to me in Farsi. Realising I did not understand, he then tried Arabic, but at this stage of my life I knew not a word of that either. He had only a smattering of English, but enough to say that his name was Ali and that he was travelling to Karbala, to visit his family. I did not try to explain that I had been in Vietnam launching what I hoped would be a career as a foreign correspondent but instead said I was a student on my way to Syria. It was not really possible to communicate much else but as the daylight faded and the coach continued its rather monotonous course westwards across semi-desert we exchanged some of the food we had each brought. He then took hold of my right hand and held on to it.

I had seen so many men holding hands, from Vietnam to Afghanistan, that I really thought nothing of this gesture at first until Ali started to gently squeeze mine. I then looked him straight in the eye. I guessed he was in his late twenties, certainly not much older, very slim and fit with an olive complexion. He smiled and squeezed my hand harder, at which point I could not help noticing through his light cotton clothes that he was sexually aroused. Such arousal had always revolted me in the case of Harold, but now I felt amused, even flattered. I smiled back and in this odd sense of communion we both dropped off to sleep.

At some hour in the middle of the night we were woken for the formalities at the Iran-Iraq border; as the one foreigner, I was taken off and led into the immigration offices on both sides of the frontier, which delayed the bus to the obvious displeasure of the driver, but as my visas were in order I was allowed to proceed. Ali smiled when I got back into my seat, took my hand once again and immediately fell asleep. In contrast, I was now wide awake. This was not just because of my exposure to the cool night air at the immigration posts had woken me up but mainly because of the groundswell of unfamiliar emotions coursing through my body. Although I was genuinely fond of my sister Hilary I had always thought I was incapable of having strong feelings towards another human being, but something weird was happening in my head that was infinitely more pleasant than the recent nightmares.

On arrival in Baghdad Ali and I checked into a hotel right by the side of the bus station, along with Ali's young cousin, who it transpired had been sitting a few seats in front of us on the bus. As my passport was now full and I still had at least 10 other countries to traverse on my way back to England, I went to the British Embassy to apply for a new one. I did not want my precious Syrian visa invalidated, so I persuaded the Embassy to afix a new passport to the front of the old one, so that both would be valid. They said this would take a few days to sort out, so back at the hotel I accepted Ali's invitation to travel with him and his cousin to Karbala to stay with his family. The young cousin, who seemed to have succumbed to a fit of jealousy because Ali was holding on to my hand while we walked round Baghdad, insisted that he sit next to Ali on the bus to Karbala, and I was relieved when we arrived in that holy city that the boy disappeared off to his own home while Ali took me to the little mudbrick house where his mother was waiting.

That afternoon he showed me the awe-inspiring Al-Abbas and Imam Hussein mosques that are the focus for Shia pilgrims for whom Karbala is the fourth most holy city after Mecca, Medina and Jerusalem. As a non-Muslim I was not allowed inside the shrines but I could sense the aura of spirituality about the place. We ate supper at a little café nearby and that night, in common with most Karbala residents in summer time, we slept on the roof of his mother's house. Seeing the moon and the stars set like diamonds in the black night sky only served to heighten the deep sense of contentment and security that I felt, lying next to Ali. He looked more like Omar Sharif than David Janssen, but laying my head on his hairy chest I felt I had found the reassurance that I had been searching for over many years. Even though I realised that it was highly likely we would never meet again after I returned to Baghdad to collect my passport, the moment was perfect. Through sign language Ali indicated that he would like to penetrate me, but I was not ready for anything like that, and he did not persist.

* * *

Everything is red. I was woken by the muezzin calling the faithful for the Fajr *prayer before dawn; then I could hear Ali's mother moving around downstairs, making preparations for breakfast. But up here on the roof, Ali is still asleep beside me, under a thin summer quilt. As the sun rises its rays ricochet off the golden domes of the twin gilded mosques of Abbas and Hussein. Karbala is stirring from its slumber.*

Ali also stirs as the first warmth of sun wakes him and he squeezes my hand. But soon he is dozing again and I am alone with my thoughts, which are jumping around in the air above us like little soap bubbles. Out of the earlier monochrome of the street below, the greens of palm trees and the ochre of mud walls gradually emerge under the red sunrise and people are starting to go about their daily chores.

Later today I will have to leave Karbala and make my way slowly across the Middle East and Europe to Oxford, where the university awaits. Already I fear it will be an anti-climax after all I have been through over the past few months. It's true, I am still a virgin – though Oxford will doubtless put paid to that – yet I have seen more than most men see in a lifetime. I am just 19, yet in some ways I feel like an old man.

But most importantly, for the first time in my life, I am truly happy. I once thought I was happy, when I was on the Greek island of Mykonos, but that was nothing like this – a happiness that fills me with great waves of emotion so that I want to cry tears of joy. I sit up and let my eyes wander from the street scene to Ali's closed eyes. I have travelled many thousands of miles in search of experience, but now I realise I was actually looking for myself. Now I have found myself I can dare to explore my emotions.

One day I will learn what I really want, not what others want for me. And I know I will find out who my Mother is.

One day I will know who I am.

193